Key stage 3

GW01255264

(H) Oxford I

Teacher's resource book 2

IAN DAWSON, CHARLES MALTMAN,
JON CRESSWELL, PETER LAURENCE,
and NEIL DEMARCO

Oxford University Press 1995

Oxford University Press
Walton Street Oxford OX2 6DP

Oxford New York
Athens Auckland Bangkok Bombay
Calcutta Cape Town Dar es Salaam Delhi
Florence Hong Kong Istanbul Karachi
Kuala Lumpur Madras Madrid Melbourne
Mexico City Nairobi Paris Singapore
Taipei Tokyo Toronto

and associated companies in
Berlin Ibadan

OXFORD is a trademark of Oxford University Press

Printed in Hong Kong

Acknowledgements:

The illustrations are by Clyde Pearson: pps 20 (x 4), 24 (x 5), 31 (x 5), 32 (x 6),
34 (x 4), 44, 48 (x 6), 49 (x 4), 67 (x 1), 98 (x 1), 110 (x 4), 111 (x 6).
Leslie Marshall: pps 20 (x 2), 43 (x 1), 61 (x 1), 64 (x 1), 75, 78, 92, 95, 98 (x 1).
Jeremy Ashcroft: pps 11, 24 (x 1), 49 (x 2), 53 (x 4), 112 (x 4).

The Publishers would also like to thank the following for permission to reproduce
photographs:

Daily Mirror pps 101, 102; Express Newspapers Ltd p.100; John Frost/Daily
Telegraph p.83; Imperial War Museum p.90 (x 3), 94; Public Records Office p.12;
Solo Syndication p.103; Solo Syndication/Daily Express pps 101, 102;
Solo Syndication/Daily Mail p.103.

Using this resource book

This is a resource book, not a teacher's guide. It therefore consists almost entirely of material that can be used by pupils, provided it is photocopied for them. There is little by way of theory. What is important to say about the series and the individual books has been said briefly. The contents deal with the National Curriculum units on The making of the United Kingdom, 1500-1750; Britain 1750 – circa 1900; and The twentieth-century world. The first resource book deals with Medieval realms, and The Roman Empire. The content is divided as follows:

5-6   **Introduction**

The approach taken by the series as a whole.

7-34   **The making of the United Kingdom, 1500-1750**

Ideas for using the pupils' book and worksheets. The worksheets include a detective exercise on The Gunpowder Plot, worksheets linked to hypothesis building and summaries of the main topics covered in the unit.

35-58   **Expansion, trade and industry, 1750-1900**

Ideas for using the pupils' book and worksheets. These include worksheets linked to hypothesis building and summaries of the main topics covered in the unit.

59-75   **Britain and the Great War**

Ideas for using the pupils' book and worksheets.

76-103   **The era of the Second World War**

Ideas for using the pupils' book and worksheets. These worksheets include a detective exercise on the massacre at Oradour, worksheets linked to hypothesis building and summaries of the main topics covered in the unit.

104-112   **Survey of British history**

A group of worksheets and picture sheets that offer the chance to revise basic knowledge of events, dates and chronology.

List of worksheets

9   The Gunpowder Plot

13   Which changes were the most important?

14   How did life change, 1500-1750?

15   How do we know about life in Britain, 1500-1750

16   The Act of Supremacy, 1534

17   The Pilgrimage of Grace, 1536

18   Religion 1500-1750 – A summary

19   The Civil War

21   Monarchs and Parliament – A summary

22   Living and working 1500-1750

23   Mary Queen of Scots

25   What to do with Mary Queen of Scots?

26   The Act of Union, 1707

27   A United Kingdom?

28   England at war – A summary

29   How do we study history?

30   What happened when?

33   Housing and costume 1500-1750

37   Did people's lives become better or worse, 1750-1900?

41   How do we know about life in Britain, 1750-1900?

42   The Atlantic slave trade

45   A woman's place

47   What happened when?

50   Living and working in the countryside – A summary

51   Living conditions in towns – A summary

52   Communications timeline

54   Would you make a good factory boss?

55   Prison conditions

56   Shops and advertising

60   How did the sides line up in 1914?

62   Why was it so difficult to launch surprise attacks?

63   Why did so many attacks fail?

65   Why did men enlist?

67   Who suffered the most casualties: officers or other ranks?

68   Why were casualties so high?

69   Why did some men turn against the war?

70   What was the most successful way of sinking a U-boat?

72   What did the war change for women?

74   How was Germany treated by the peace?

77   Hypothesis grid: Why did war not break out before September 1939?

78   Czechoslovakia 1939 – choosing war or peace?

80   Germany and the League of Nations in the 1930s

81   Hypothesis grid: Could the Axis powers have won the Second World War?

82   Dunkirk, May 1940

85   The Battle of Britain

87   The Engima code and the bombing of Coventry

88   What was the war like?

89   How do we know about the Second World War?

90   Why did men fight?

91   Operation Barbarossa

94   The treatment of conscientious objectors

95   Why Germany lost the Second World War

96   Pearl Harbor

97   Massacre at Oradour

100   What happened when?

104   People and events in British history – Sheet A

105   People and events in British history – Sheet B

106   Early modern Britain

107   The Industrial Revolution

108   The modern world

Oxford history study units – the series and its approach

1 The general approach

National Curriculum History involves the study of the content of history (the Programmes of Study) and the skills and concepts used by historians (the Attainment Target elements). Oxford history study units bring the two elements together by creating in each book an historical investigation which allows pupils to follow the general process of studying history (shown below).

General approach to historical investigation

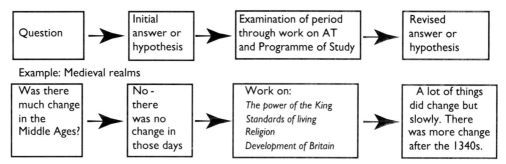

At the end of each topic pupils will be able to see that they have developed their knowledge of events and issues by comparing their final answers with their initial answers. They will also have developed their understanding of the concepts and skills through using them to build their answer. This approach is open-ended and will, therefore, help pupils to see that the study of history is continuous, producing revised and new understandings rather than permanent answers. It can also be tackled by pupils of a range of levels of ability.

2 Key questions

Each book is, therefore, built around a single key question or tackles a series of related questions. For the British topics the key questions are:

Medieval realms	Did life change in the Middle Ages?
The making of the United Kingdom	Which change was the most important?
Expansion, trade and industry	Did changes make life better or worse?

One specific advantage of these questions is that they all deal with the idea of change, allowing contrasts across the period 1066-1900 and helping to give some unity to the study of British history.

The advantages of this approach are:

a) Questions give unity and prevent history fragmenting into a series of one- off lessons, double pages or lines in the NC document.

b) If pupils are encouraged to suggest answers at the beginning of the topic (or are given a handful of sources on which to base suggestions) then they have a hypothesis of their own to investigate. This may add to motivation by personalizing the study and at the end allows pupils to measure what they have learned by comparing their final answers to the key question(s) with their initial answer.

c) Key questions are devised to fit in with the Attainment Target, thus ensuring that AT questions arise naturally out of the work and are not an add-on extra. Thus the British topic questions allow teachers to develop pupils' understanding of change/ continuity and causation as a natural part of the investigation.

d) Questions are as open-ended as possible, allowing pupils to pursue them according to their own abilities. Questions such as 'What was it like living in the Roman Empire?' allow pupils to bring in a number of variables. The answer is 'It depends' – on who you were, where you lived, when you lived etc. Pupils of different abilities will be able to pursue the same question but in differing degrees of depth.

e) This approach of 'question – hypothesis – evidence – reconsider hypothesis' is good history, introducing pupils to the general historical process as well as its constituent skills, concepts and knowledge. It may also help pupils to ask their own questions and to see asking questions as a crucial part of 'doing history'.

f) Questions allow you to take control of content and use it for a purpose rather than being at the mercy of a check–list of events and topics which must be covered but in unspecified depth. Here the appropriate depth is that needed for pupils to add to and develop their answer to the key question for the topic.

g) Key questions allow topics to be linked together, perhaps using one as a case-study to test conclusions reached in another topic. For example *Castles and cathedrals* investigates the following questions: Why were castles and cathedrals needed? Were medieval builders skilful? Was life comfortable in castles and cathedrals? Did castles and cathedrals change in the Middle Ages? Each of these questions would link to Medieval realms and allow Castles and cathedrals to be used as a case-study testing conclusions reached in *Medieval realms*.

National Curriculum changes

Oxford History Study Units fit comfortably into the post-Dearing framework of National Curriculum history. The central approaches of the series are unchanged, remaining central to effective teaching and learning as well as providing the opportunity to save time without losing coherence. Time can still be taken to set up investigations and to establish pupils' prior understandings of periods and AT elements, but one lesson should suffice. Where OHSU creates opportunities is in allowing groups of pupils to investigate different aspects of a topic and using their conclusions to create an overall answer. For example, in *The Making of the United Kingdom*, different groups can investigate events in Scotland and Ireland but their work is given unity by the overall question of whether England's power was growing. Other examples can be found in the guides to using the books in this Resource Book.

In addition, *Expansion, Trade and Industry* provides an ideal outline investigation of British life 1750-1900, creating the framework for a local study in which the book's conclusions about progress can be tested. Similarly the books *Britain and the Great War* and *The Era of the Second World War* provide a framework for the study of twentieth-century history. They combine work on the events and nature of each conflict with studies of their social consequences. Either wartime events or social background would set the background for schools' chosen depth studies.

Using *The making of the United Kingdom*

In keeping with the overall approach of the series *The making of the United Kingdom* is structured as an investigation, focusing on the question: 'Which changes were the most important for the people of Britain?' This question can be explored and answered at a variety of levels, depending on pupils' ability. The question is introduced on pages 7-8 where pupils are invited to suggest an initial answer. Each chapter then has its own central question linked to the issue of change and continuity so that the initial hypothesis can be added to and amended at the end of each chapter. Page 76 repeats the initial question so that pupils can compare their final answer with their first ideas. This comparison is important, in building pupils' confidence and awareness of what they have learned.

Other features of the book are:
   a   The opportunity to speed progress by dividing work amongst groups of pupils who each pursue the same question but through different content. Examples are given below.
   b   Opportunities for recording pupils' understanding of Attainment Target elements are signposted by question headings e.g., Changes, Evidence etc. A full list of headings and page numbers of exercises is on page 2.
   c   Explicit questions on the process of studying history on page 77.
   d   A survey of British history from 1066-1750 (pages 78-9) to remind pupils of last year's work.

The following chapter by chapter notes may assist planning and show links to material in this Resource book.

Chapter 1
   a   pages 4-5 offer the chance to see if pupils have heard of any events from this period and to provide a first outline of events.
   b   pages 6-7 draw an overall contrast between the medieval period and early modern Britain and introduce ideas of change.
   c   page 8 provides the opportunity to establish a first answer to the book's main question, using a grid (see also Resource book sheet 13). At this stage it may also be useful to find out how much pupils know and understand about the period before starting the topic. Resource book sheets 14-15 will provide the basis for this diagnosis. Sheet 30 used in conjunction with Resource cards 1-12 will help pupils develop their knowledge of the ordering of events and will be most effective if used briefly and frequently.

Chapter 2 investigates religious changes and their impact. The text and evidence on pages 9-17 explains the changes and continuities and the reasons for them. The summary on page 18 pulls these issues together, allowing the initial hypothesis to be extended. Work on the variety of perspectives is particularly important to gain an insight into attitudes towards religion. Supporting worksheets are Resource book sheets 16-18.

Chapter 3 looks at the changing balance of power between the monarch and Parliament. It looks at what changed and the causes and consequences of these changes. The exercises on kings and queens allow the pupils to explore the nature of power. Some of this could be done as group work, where groups of pupils take one or two monarchs and assess them, then reporting their findings back to the class. This could lead to a discussion based on the differing requirements of kingship in 1500 and 1760. The grid on page 23 enables the pupils to record the results of their investigation of what changed and the significance of those changes through pages 23-7.

Pages 28-9 look at the various factors which contributed to change in the power of the monarch and Parliament. In pages 30-1 the students are asked to consider whether or not these changes were important and, if so, for whom. The detective exercise on the Gunpowder Plot enables the students to explore certain problems of evidence (sheet 9).

Chapter 4 is a case-study of the English Civil War. It enables the students to explore a major event in some detail using contemporary source material, to examine the views of people in the past and their motives. It also enables students to see how interpretations of the role of a particular individual come about. Students could approach this chapter as a decision-making exercise. After reading pages 32 and 33 they could, individually or in groups, decide whom they would support and why. This could then be recorded. As they work through the rest of the chapter they could reconsider their decision at key stages such as the execution of the king and the Restoration and decide whether or not they should change their minds. A sequencing exercise in the Resource book (sheets 19-20) can be used to reinforce ideas about chronology and causation.

Chapter 5 Examines daily life and focuses on work on evidence. In order to give pupils the chance to make sense of a group of sources for themselves, sources are provided on pages 42-3 without guiding questions. A summary then follows, together with questions on the value of the sources as evidence, on page 44. The same pattern is repeated on pages 45-9. It is hoped that this arrangement will allow pupils to develop ideas independently if they are able to do so. Supporting worksheets are Resource book sheets 22 and 33-4.

Chapter 6 looks at the steps towards the formation of the United Kingdom and asks to what extent union was achieved during this period. By looking at the opinions of contemporaries and historians this chapter provides a good vehicle for identifying a diversity of views. Students could begin by copying the grid on page 57 into their books and using it to record what kind of union was achieved and how it was achieved. Group work can be provided if the students are divided into groups representing the different nationalities who could evaluate the process of union. A sequencing exercise and a decision-making exercise enable students to look more closely at the problems created by Mary Queen of Scots (sheets 23-5) and a further decision-making exercise looks at the Act of Union of 1707 from a Scottish point of view (sheet 26).

Chapter 7 The key question for this chapter is 'Why did England go to war?' The chapter focuses on the causes and consequences of England's involvement with European countries and with the wider world. The students would find it useful to keep a record of their findings on a grid like the one on page 68.

Chapter 8 Acts as the conclusion, addressing the main themes of change and continuity, allowing pupils to pull together their overall ideas by returning to the questions on page 8. Page 76 offers an outline set of answers for pupils to compare with their own ideas. Page 77 again looks explicitly at the process of history so that pupils are as aware of how we study as what we study. Pages 78-9 offer an overview of British history from 1066 and questions that allow pupils to look back over earlier work as well as at this unit.

In November 1605 Guy Fawkes was arrested in a cellar underneath the Houses of Parliament. He was surrounded by barrels of gunpowder. He was tortured and confessed to having tried, with a group of fellow plotters, blow up the king and the members of Parliament assembled for the State Opening of Parliament.

The traditional story

During the reign of Elizabeth I many laws had been passed against Catholics. They were not allowed to have services of their own, they had to pay fines for not going to Protestant church services and their priests, if caught, could be executed. Because of this some Catholics had plotted to murder Elizabeth and make her Catholic cousin, Mary Queen of Scots, queen in her place. When Elizabeth died and James I became king Catholics hoped that he would be sympathetic to their cause because he was the son of Mary Queen of Scots. Although James did not hate Catholics he knew that many English people did, including his own chief minister, Lord Salisbury. The laws against Catholics were made even harsher.

In 1604 a group of Catholic gentlemen led by Robert Catesby decided to do something to help their fellow Catholics. They planned to kill the king, Salisbury and the members of Parliament whom they blamed for all their troubles. The best time to do this would be when the king opened the new Parliament on 5 November, 1605. The ceremony would take place in the House of Lords and be attended by the king, the lords and the members of the House of Commons. At first the plotters rented a house near Parliament and tried to dig a tunnel under the House of Lords. This was not successful but they were able to rent a cellar under the House of Lords. They filled it with gunpowder and employed a Catholic ex-soldier and explosives expert, Guy Fawkes, to set off the explosion.

One of the plotters, Francis Tresham, wrote to his cousin, Lord Monteagle, warning him to stay away from the ceremony. Monteagle showed the letter to Salisbury who had the cellars and buildings surrounding the House of Lords searched. Guy Fawkes was caught. Some of the plotters were killed when resisting arrest in Worcestershire. Others were tried for treason and hanged, drawn and quartered in January 1606.

Some historians have thought that there are problems with this story. They think that the plot could not have got as far as it did without some help from the government. The sources and information will help you to investigate the story of the Gunpowder Plot and to test the different ideas against the evidence. It is your job to work out what questions to ask and to decide on the answers.

The questions below will help you to think about how we investigate history.

Before you start:

1 Make a list of the questions you want to ask about the Gunpowder Plot

As you investigate the sources:

2 What problems are there in finding answers to your questions?

When you have finished:

3 Which questions were the easiest to answer? Why?

4 Which questions were the hardest to answer? Why?

5 Why might historians have different answers to some questions?

Some other important points

- Gunpowder was stored in the Tower of London and all sales were controlled by the government. Detailed records were kept of how much had been sold and to whom. The Tower records for 1604 are missing. They could have been lost or destroyed.
- The cellar under the Houses of Parliament rented to the plotters belonged to a friend of Lord Salisbury. He died suddenly on 5 November, cause unknown.
- When the Gunpowder Plot was revealed there was a great deal of ill feeling towards Catholics. The government became more popular and was able to pass even harsher laws against Catholics.

Information about the sources

Francis Tresham. One of the plotters. He was not arrested until 12 December, after the trial. He was imprisoned in the Tower of London. He died there of a mysterious illness on 23 December.

Guy Fawkes. One of the plotters. He was an ex-soldier and explosives expert. He was hired by the other plotters to set off the explosion. When he was caught he gave his name as Johnson. He was tortured and made a confession under torture. He was hanged, drawn and quartered in January 1606.

Thomas Winter. One of the plotters. He was wounded in the right shoulder when he was captured on 8 November. His confession was used as evidence at the trial. Although the writing looks like his there are doubts about it. On 12 November he could not sign his own statement because of his wound. At the trial only a copy of the confession was produced, not the original

Lord Salisbury. James I's chief minister. He hated Catholics.

Source A

Guy Fawkes's confession

He said he did not intend to set fire to the fuse until the king came into the House, and then he intended to do it so the gunpowder might more surely blow up a quarter of an hour later.

Source B

A plan of the Houses of Parliament and the surrounding area

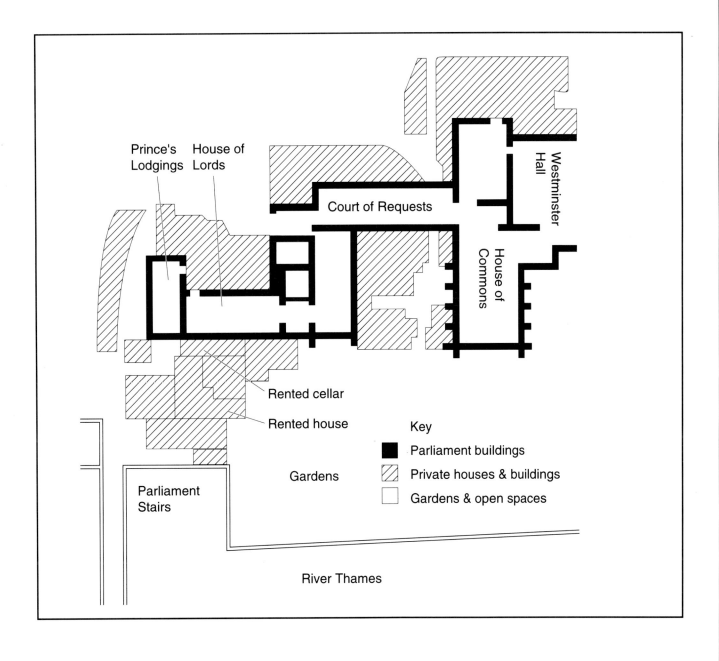

Prince's Lodgings
House of Lords
Court of Requests
Westminster Hall
House of Commons
Rented cellar
Rented house
Gardens
Parliament Stairs

Key
■ Parliament buildings
▨ Private houses & buildings
□ Gardens & open spaces

River Thames

Source C

Letter allegedly written by Francis Tresham to Lord Monteagle

my lord, out of the love I beare to some of youere frendz i have a caer of yoer preservacion therfor i would advyse yowe as youe tender yoer lyf to devise some excuse to shift of yoer attendance at this parleament for god and man hathe concurred to punishe the wickednes of this tyme and thinke not slightlye of this advertisment but retyere youre self into youre contri wheare yowe may expect the event in safti for thowye theare be no apparance of anni stir yet i say they shall receyve a terrible blowe this parleament and yet they shall not seie who hurts them this councel is not to be a contemned becaus it maye do yowe good and can do yowe no harme for the danger is passed as soon as yowe have burnt the letter and i hope god will give yowe the grace to make good use of it to whose holy profeccion i commend yowe

(I would advise you as you tender (value) your life to devise some excuse to shift of your attendance at this Parliament for god and man have concurred to punish the wickedness of this time and think not slightly of this advertisement (warning) but retire yourself into your country where you may expect the event in safety for though they be no appearance of any stir yet I say they shall receive a terrible blow this Parliament and yet they shall not see who hurts them)

Source D

Letter from Lord Salisbury to the English Ambassador in Brussels, 9 November 1605

It has pleased Almighty God to discover the most cruel and detestable plot. The plot was to kill the King, Queen, Prince, Council, Clergy, Judges and the principal gentlemen by secretly putting a great quantity of gunpowder into a cellar under Parliament, and so to have blown all up at a clap., God out of his mercy and just revenge, allowed it to be discovered. The main plotter is one Johnson, a Yorkshire man and servant to Thomas Percy. This Percy had, about a year and a half ago, hired a house by Parliament, from which he had access to the cellar to store his wood and coal. He is a Catholic, and so is his man Johnson. Into this cellar Johnson had carried a great quantity of powder, all of which he had cunningly covered with firewood. On Tuesday at midnight, as he was busy to prepare his things for explosion, he was caught in the place itself. There was found some fine powder to make a fuse. He would have saved himself from the blow by some half an hour.

Source E

Letter from an Italian visitor, 1605

Those that have practical experience of the way in which things are done hold it as certain that there has been foul play and that some of the Council secretly spun a web to entangle these poor gentlemen.

Source F

Thomas Winter's confession

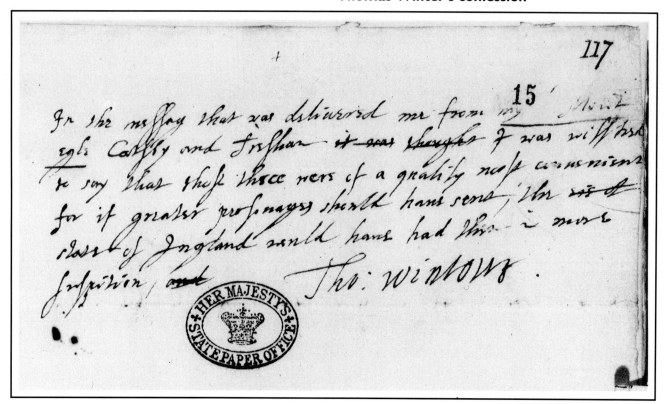

Which changes were the most important?

On the left of the grid are five topics you will investigate. Fill the grid in now with your first ideas. Keep the grid and compare it with your ideas after you have studied each topic. Have your ideas changed?

a   Complete column 1 now. If you think a change was very important give it 9 or 10 out of 10.

b   After each chapter complete columns 2-7.

c   At the end of your study column 5 will show you which change you think was most important.

	1 *First answer* Was it an important change? (1-10)	2 Were many people affected by the changes?	3 Were the effects of the changes long-lasting?	4 Were the changes rapid or slow?	5 *Revised answer* Was it an important change? (1-10)	6 Did these changes help to unite Britain?	7 Do these changes still affect us today?
Religion							
Everyday life							
The power of the monarch							
England's power in Britain							
British involvement abroad							

How did life change between 1500 and 1750?

Below are nine statements about how life changed between 1500 and 1750. Tick the boxes next to the statements you think are true. Rewrite the false statements at the bottom of the page so they are correct.

☐	1	The total population stayed the same between 1500 and 1750.
☐	2	Nearly everyone still lived by farming but towns were growing quickly by 1750.
☐	3	Plagues and diseases disappeared thanks to discoveries about germs and hygiene.
☐	4	The standard of living of ordinary people (their diet, clothing and housing) grew worse.
☐	5	Travel became much faster and easier thanks to canals and railways.
☐	6	People stayed very religious.
☐	7	Parliament became much more powerful but the king was still very important in 1750.
☐	8	England won complete control over the rest of Britain.
☐	9	British people began to settle in colonies all over the world and Britain's foreign trade became very much larger.

Here is a list of sources that historians might use to find out about life in the past:

☐ tape-recordings   ☐ photographs

☐ the homes of the poor   ☐ records of law cases

☐ poems and songs   ☐ paintings

☐ colour films   ☐ the homes of the rich

☐ autobiographies by famous people   ☐ black and white films

1   Tick the sources that tell us about life between 1500 and 1750?

2   Can you think of any other sources that you could use to find out about this period?

3   Choose two sources. Explain what you might learn from them.

4   Choose one kind of source. List the questions you would ask to check if it was a reliable source.

The Act of Supremacy, 1534

King Henry VIII has decided that his marriage to Catherine of Aragon was unlawful. The Pope has refused to recognize this so Henry has decided to make himself Head of the Church of England. Archbishop Cranmer has pronounced Henry free to marry Anne Boleyn.

Parliament has passed a law declaring Henry to be Head of the Church and Anne Boleyn to be Queen of England. Included in this law is an order that all government officials, teachers, lawyers and clergymen have to take an oath agreeing that Henry is Head of the Church and that Anne Boleyn is Queen.

Your friend, Sir Thomas More, is Chancellor of England. He knows that he will be asked to take the oath and has discussed with you what he should do. Before you decide what advice you should give him, consider the following points.

1   You know that Sir Thomas does not believe that Henry has the right to make himself Head of the Church.
2   It is the duty of all Englishmen to obey the king. Both you and Sir Thomas have always been loyal to King Henry.
3   You believe that someone who goes against the rules of the Church risks going to hell when they die.
4   King Henry has made no other changes in the Church. He has upheld the traditional beliefs and has made no changes in the church services.
5   Refusal of the oath will mean the loss of his job and possibly execution for Sir Thomas.
6   You have heard that Sir Thomas's friend, John Fisher, Bishop of Rochester, has decided to refuse the oath.

King Henry VIII takes control of the Church

1532   Annates Act – No more taxes to be paid to the Pope.

1533   Appeals Act – No more appeals from English church courts to Rome.

1533   Archbishop Cranmer grants Henry his divorce from Catherine of Aragon. Henry marries Anne Boleyn.

1534   Act of Supremacy – Henry made Supreme Head of the Church of England.

1534   Act of Succession – Henry and Anne's children to succeed to the throne. All important people to take oath declaring they accept this.

In the Middle Ages many men and women devoted their lives to God by becoming monks or nuns. Many monasteries helped the local people by feeding the poor, looking after the sick and providing schools for the children. On the other hand many monasteries had become very rich through running farms and industries. These often provided employment for local people, especially in the north of England.

King Henry VIII was short of money. He had defied the authority of the Pope and expected the Catholic countries of Europe to attack England. He needed money to pay for the army and navy necessary to defend the country. The King and his chief adviser, Thomas Cromwell, decided that hey could raise this money by closing all the monasteries and confiscating all their property.

In the north of England most people were deeply attached to the old ways of the Catholic Church and were unhappy about the religious changes that were beginning to happen as a result of King Henry taking control of the Church. They were also deeply worried because the closing of the monasteries could mean that they would lose their jobs, that the sick would not be cared for and that children would not be educated.

Your lord has been invited to join the Pilgrimage of Grace against the closing of the monasteries. He has been told that the King is not really responsible for the changes but has come under the influence of bad advisers. Your lord has called together his tenants to ask for their support.

Before making your decision consider the following points:

1 You do some work for the local monastery. You could lose this work if the monastery is closed.
2 If the rebellion is unsuccessful, you could be executed as a traitor.
3 All the other lords in the area have decided to join the rebellion and have been supported by their tenants.
4 It is possible that the king himself has decided to close the monasteries. The rebellion would then be against the authority of the king himself. You are reluctant to commit treason.
5 You are loyal to your lord. If you went against him he might deprive you of your land and you and your family would starve.
6 The monks have always been good to you and your family but you have heard rumours of scandalous goings-on in the monastery.

Some of the things the 'pilgrims' wanted:

- The Pope to be restored as Head of the Church.
- Monasteries which had been closed to be reopened.
- Thomas Cromwell, the king's chief minister and the man responsible for the closure of the monasteries, to be punished.
- Other reforms such as a better system of taxes.

Religion 1500-1750 – A summary

How important was religion for the people of Britain? This sheet will help you summarize your work on religion.

1 Fill in the grid below, putting examples of the effects of changes into the boxes.

2 Did everyone think that religion was very important for everyone? Give an example to support your answer.

3 Do you think that religion had helped to unite the people of Britain by 1750 or had it helped to cause more problems?

4 Do you think that the religious changes of 1500-1750 still affect us today?

The effects of religious changes	
A Many people were executed or imprisoned	
B Civil wars and changes of monarch	
C People emigrated to worship freely	
D Churches looked different; monasteries were closed	
E Wars with other countries	
F Differences between England, Scotland, Wales and Ireland	

The Civil War

You need Sequencing cards A-F.

1   Look at cards A-F. Put them in chronological order. Then write their letters in chronological order in these boxes.

☐   ☐   ☐   ☐   ☐   ☐

2   The dates below are the dates of important events in the Civil War. Write in the events above opposite the starred dates. Then complete the chart from your knowlege of the Civil War.

1640 _____

* 1642 _____

* 1643 _____

1644 _____

* 1645 _____

1646 _____

* 1648 _____

* 1649 _____

1658 _____

* 1660 _____

3   Use the table above and your own knowledge to write your own account of the events of 1640 to 1660.

A New Model Army defeats Charles's forces at Battle of Naseby

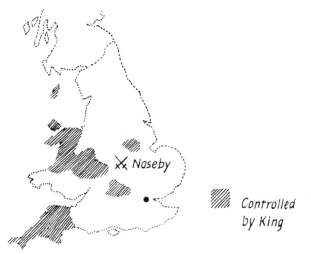

B King Charles I raises his standard at Nottingham

C Coronation of King Charles II

D King Charles I held prisoner on the Isle of Wight

E The execution of King Charles I

F Charles launches attack on south-east England

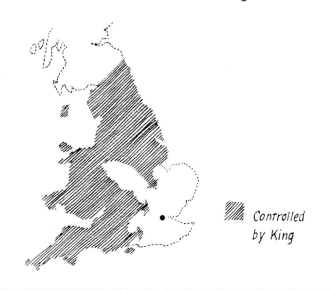

Monarchs and Parliament – A summary

The information and questions on this sheet will help you to summarize your work on the power of monarch and Parliament during the period. How and why did the balance of power between monarch and Parliament change?

1   Draw a pair of scales to show the balance of power between Henry VII and his Parliaments. Explain in your own words why Henry VII was more powerful than Parliament.

2   Draw a pair of scales to show the balance of power between George II and his Parliaments. Which do you think was the more powerful in 1760, king or Parliament? Explain your answer carefully.

3   Do you think the Civil War was a major turning point in the power of monarch and Parliament?

4   What role do you think religion played in changing the balance of power between monarch and Parliament?

5   What role do you think war played in changing the balance of power between monarch and Parliament?

6   At what stage do you think Parliament began to have more power than the monarch?

- King Henry VII was very powerful. He was very rich and did not need to ask for taxes. He only called Parliament occasionally.

- Henry VIII, Edward VI, Mary I and Elizabeth I used Parliament to make religious changes. Parliaments then believed that they had a right to control religious policy.

- King Charles I ruled for eleven years without Parliament. Then he fought a war against Parliament and was eventually executed. England was without a king for eleven years.

- King Charles II was made king in 1660, after the Civil War, without any conditions. When he had enough money he could rule without Parliament.

- England was often at war. This cost a lot of money and forced the king or queen to go to Parliament for more money. This gave Parliament the chance to try to influence the monarch's decisions. In the reign of William III war became so expensive that Parliament had to meet every year to provide enough money.

- Kings George I and George II spent a lot of time in Hanover. They had to rely on ministers to make many of the day to day decisions previously made by the monarch. These ministers had to be approved by Parliament.

- Even in 1750 the king had considerable patronage (the power to give well-paid jobs and titles to his supporters) and used this to persuade members of Parliament to support his policies.

This sheet will help you to decide whether there was much change in daily life between 1500 and 1750.

1 Look at the detail below.

    a If you had the chance to go back in time which period would you choose to live in?

    b Which of these factors were most important in reaching your decision?

- housing, diet and clothing
- religious changes
- wages and prices
- wars and invasions
- others?

    c Would you choose a different period depending on whether you were rich or poor?

2 Do you think there was:
    a a lot
    b some
    c no change in the way people lived between 1500 and 1750?
    Explain the reasons for your answer.

1500-1550	1550-1600	1600-1650	1650-1700	1700-1750
Henry VIII closed the monasteries when he broke away from the Roman Catholic Church. Prices were rising and Henry's wars made inflation worse. There were rebellions in 1536 and 1549 but no more civil wars. More and more people were going to school.	England had to fight off the Spanish invasion in 1588. Bad harvests made inflation worse, especially in the 1550s and 1590s. The country's religion changed from Protestant to Catholic and then back to Protestant. Some people were executed for their beliefs. Housing began to improve rapidly.	There was a long civil war and the king was executed. England was not a powerful country abroad. English armies fought in Scotland and Ireland. Living standards were improving as people had a better diet, housing and clothing.	There was more danger of civil war and disputes over religion. The plague and Great Fire hit London in the 1660s. Science was improving and education developing still faster. Fashions changed dramatically when Charles II returned as king in 1660.	Industries were developing and towns were growing. Plagues were still dangerous and killed many people. There were long wars with France, and Britain built up an empire England and Scotland were united but Protestants in Ireland took nearly all the land over from Catholics.

Mary Queen of Scots

In 1542 Mary Queen of Scots became Queen of Scotland on the death of her father when she was only one week old. She spent the last 19 years of her life as a prisoner in England and was executed at the age of 45. Mary spent her childhood in France, where she married the son of the French king. A year later her husband became king but he died shortly afterwards and Mary was forced to return to Scotland. Mary, a Catholic, did not find it easy to be queen of a Protestant country like Scotland. She married her cousin Lord Darnley but they quarrelled. When he was murdered Mary was blamed. She married the Earl of Bothwell who was believed to have been the murderer. The Scots made her infant son king in her place and Mary fled to England. Elizabeth I was frightened by the presence of a Catholic heir to the throne and kept her prisoner. There were several Catholic plots to make Mary queen of England instead of Elizabeth. Mary became involved in a plot led by Sir Anthony Babington in 1586 but English government spies found out and Mary was tried and sentenced to death.

You need Sequencing cards G-L.

1 Look at cards G-L. Put them in chronological order. Then write their letters in chronological order in these boxes.

☐ ☐ ☐ ☐ ☐ ☐

2 The dates below are the dates of important events in the life of Mary Queen of Scots. Write in the events above opposite the starred dates. Then complete the chart from your knowledge of her life.

	1542	_____
✱	1548	_____
✱	1558	_____
	1559	_____
✱	1561	_____
	1565	_____
✱	1567	_____
✱	1568	_____
	1586	_____
✱	1587	_____

3 Some people have seen Mary as a wicked woman who murdered her husband and plotted to kill Elizabeth I. Others have seen her as a tragic woman, victim of circumstances beyond her control. Which of these views do you agree with? Explain your answer fully.

Sequencing cards G-L

G The murder of Lord Darnley

H The young queen is sent to France

I The execution of Mary Queen of Scots

J Mary marries Prince Francis of France

K Mary is held prisoner at Tutbury Castle in England

L Mary returns to Scotland from France

In 1568 Mary Queen of Scots fled from Scotland to England. She threw herself at the mercy of Queen Elizabeth I. Elizabeth was faced with a difficult decision. She did not want Mary in England where a Catholic heir to the throne would be a threat to Elizabeth herself. To send Mary back to Scotland, however, would be to send her to almost certain death. If Elizabeth sent Mary to France she would probably try to persuade the French to attack England. In the end Elizabeth decided to keep Mary a prisoner in England.

During the 19 years that Mary was a prisoner a number of plots were hatched to kill Elizabeth and make Mary queen in her place. At first there was no evidence to link Mary with these plots but some leading Englishmen believed that she was involved. After many years in prison Mary became involved in a plot organized by Sir Anthony Babington, a Catholic gentleman. She sent Babington coded messages not knowing that the code was known to the English government. Mary was tried for treason, found guilty and sentenced to death. The sentence could only be carried out, however, with the approval of Queen Elizabeth.

The Queen has asked you and her other councillors to advise her on the best course of action.

Before giving your advice and the reasons for it, consider the following points:

1   Mary is a queen. To have a queen executed would give a bad example to others. It might encourage others to try to murder Elizabeth.

2   As long as Mary lives some Catholics will plot to kill Elizabeth and put Mary on the throne. They hope that Mary will make England a Catholic country again.

3   Mary has powerful friends abroad. If Elizabeth has Mary executed then France or Spain or both may decide to attack England.

4   Some evidence exists that Mary was involved in the murder of her husband. If this is correct then she is not worth protecting.

5   Mary is Elizabeth's cousin. The queen does not want to be seen to kill close members of her own family.

6   Parliament has been pressing Elizabeth to have Mary executed. The Members feel that if one of the Catholic plots were to succeed many Protestant Englishmen would be killed.

Source

(Extract from coded letter from Mary Queen of Scots to Sir Anthony Babington)

Everything be prepared, and the forces both within and without (in England and abroad) being ready, then you must set the six gentlemen to work; give order that when their design is accomplished, I may in some way be got away from here and that all your forces shall be set in the field to receive me while we wait for foreign help.

The Act of Union, 1707

After the Civil War Charles II became King of Scotland as well as King of England. Scotland had its own Parliament and was ruled separately from England. Most Scots were happy to be ruled by a king of their own ruling family, the Stuarts. When the English deposed James II in favour of William of Orange and his wife Mary, the Scottish Parliament accepted them as king and queen. Many Scots, however, wanted to preserve their independence from England. In the reign of Queen Anne, when the English decided that her heir should be the Protestant prince George of Hanover, the Scottish Parliament proclaimed the right to choose Anne's Catholic brother, James, instead. The English believed that this would lead to a permanent break and possible war so they proposed that England and Scotland should become one country.

You are a member of the Scottish Parliament and you have to decide whether or not to accept the Act of Union which will unite your country with England.

Before you make your decision consider the following points.

1   Scotland is a very poor country. You might be better off if you joined with much richer England.

2   Some Scottish industries would suffer from competition with more successful English ones.

3   Scotland would be able to trade with the English empire, including North America.

4   Union with England would mean less trade with France, Scotland's traditional ally.

5   Protestant George would be preferable as king to Catholic James.

6   English Protestantism is very different from Scottish Protestantism. You are afraid of English interference in your Church.

7   You are afraid that Scotland will be swallowed up by a richer and more powerful England and that Scotland will lose her independence and identity.

8   If you vote against union there might be war between England and Scotland.

The Stuart Succession

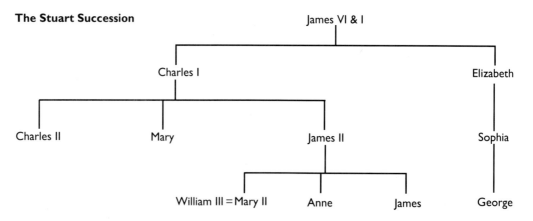

A United Kingdom?

The information and questions on this sheet will help you to summarize your work on the making of the United Kingdom. In particular you will be able to say how union was brought about in each case, how successful it was and to what extent we can talk about a united kingdom in 1750.

1   Copy and complete the diagram below by including details of the relationship of Scotland, Ireland and Wales to England in 1500.

2   Make a similar diagram for 1750 showing how Scotland, Ireland and Wales were tied to England. Call it 'A United Kingdom? 1750'.

3   How far did force have to be used to bring about union with England in:

    a   Scotland
    b   Ireland
    c   Wales?

4   How far do you think the people of each country had accepted the union by 1750?

    a   Scotland
    b   Ireland
    c   Wales
    d   England

5   How united do you think Britain was in 1750?

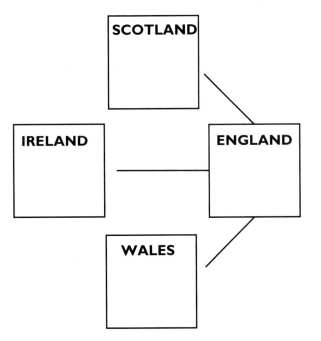

The Four Kingdoms in 1500

In 1500 Wales and parts of Ireland had been colonized by the English but Scotland was still an independent country, often at war with England.

When England and Scotland were united, the Scottish people kept many of their traditional laws and customs.

The Tudor monarchs used their Welsh origins to make their rule in Wales easier.

The English fought many wars in Ireland before achieving victory in 1691.

When James VI of Scotland became James I of England he was not able to unite the two countries. Some Scots continued to resist union until 1745.

In 1750 Ireland was ruled by a small minority of Protestants of English descent. Most of the people were Catholics of Irish descent.

England at War – A Summary

The information and questions on this sheet will help you to summarize your work on England at war. You will look at why England went to war at the beginning of this period and explain how and why the reasons for going to war had changed by 1750.

1 What reasons did Henry VIII have for going to war against France and Scotland?
2 What were the causes of war between England and Spain during the reign of Elizabeth I?
3 What did the English and Dutch fight about in the mid-seventeenth century?
4 Why did England and France become rivals again in the late-seventeenth and eighteenth centuries?
5 Copy and complete the diagram below by putting ticks in the boxes for the most important reasons for war in each period. What do you notice from this diagram about the reasons for going to war?

	Personal glory	Royal claims	Religion	Trade	Overseas empire	Self defence
Henry VIII						
Elizabeth I						
Commonwealth and Charles II						
Late seventeenth and eighteenth centuries						

- In 1500 the decision to go to war was made by the king.
- In the Middle Ages English kings had fought wars in France because they thought they had the right to be kings of France as well as England.
- During the sixteenth and seventeenth centuries the Dutch, English, French, Portuguese and Spanish had explored parts of America, Africa and the Far East. They established trading bases and colonies in these places and tried to keep other nations out.
- The religious changes of the sixteenth century brought about conflict between countries trying to impose their religious ideas on others.
- From the middle of the seventeenth century control of relations with other countries was passing from the king to Parliament. By 1750 Parliament had almost complete control over the decision to go to war.
- In the late sixteenth and early seventeenth centuries Spain was the most powerful country in Europe. In the late seventeenth century France tried to become the most powerful country in Europe. Smaller countries like England would sometimes form alliances to resist domination by the most powerful country.

How do we study history?

These four boxes show the stages of an investigation. Now you have finished your investigation can you describe what you did? Use these headings as guidelines. Explain in each box what you did and how your answer changed.

Stage 1
Start with a question

Which of these changes was the most important?

Stage 3
Investigate what happened in the past

That was more important than I thought

Stage 2
Suggest an answer even if you aren't sure

Changes in daily life were probably the most important

Stage 4
Revise your first answer or hypothesis

That first answer wasn't bad but this is better...

What happened when?

You need Sequencing cards 1-12 to help you with these activities.

1 Look at cards 1, 2, 3 and 8. Put them into chronological order. Then write their numbers in chronological order in these boxes.

☐ ☐ ☐ ☐

2 Write the number of the cards above in the starred boxes below. Then look at cards 4, 7, 10, 11. Put all eight cards into chronological order, then add the new numbers into the empty boxes.

* ☐ ☐ ☐ * ☐ * ☐ ☐ ☐ * ☐

3 Write the numbers of the cards above in the starred boxes below. Then look at the rest of the cards and put all twelve cards into chronological order. Write the new numbers in the empty boxes.

* ☐ * ☐ * ☐ ☐ * ☐ ☐ * ☐ * ☐ ☐ ☐ * ☐ * ☐

4 The dates below are the dates of eight of the events on your cards. Which event fits which date?

1649 _____

1485 _____

1660 _____

1605 _____

1536 _____

1588 _____

1688 _____

1707 _____

5 What are the dates of the other four events?

☐ ☐ ☐ ☐

6 Find out when these events happened.

a The Battle of Marston Moor   ☐

b Isaac Newton discovered gravity   ☐

c Samuel Pepys began his diary   ☐

d The Battle of Naseby   ☐

e Francis Drake's voyage around the world   ☐

f Bonnie Prince Charlie's defeat at Culloden   ☐

1 THE GUNPOWDER PLOT

Catholic plotters, including Guy Fawkes, attempted to blow up James I.

2 THE EXECUTION OF CHARLES I

Charles was executed, bringing the Civil War to an end.

3 THE BATTLE OF BOSWORTH

When Henry VII killed Richard III.

4 THE RESTORATION

Charles II became king, ending eleven years without a king.

5 THE BATTLE OF BLENHEIM

The Duke of Marlborough's greatest victory over France.

6 THE MAYFLOWER

The voyage of the Pilgrim Fathers to America, seeking religious freedom.

7 THE SPANISH ARMADA

Spain's invasion force was beaten by the weather and the English navy.

8 GEORGE I

The first German king of England from Hanover.

9 THE GLORIOUS REVOLUTION

James II was forced to give up the throne. He was succeeded by Protestants William and Mary.

10 THE DISSOLUTION OF THE MONASTERIES

Henry VIII and Thomas Cromwell closed all the monasteries after they had founded the Church of England.

11 ENGLAND AND SCOTLAND UNITED

Parliament passed an Act making the two countries into one.

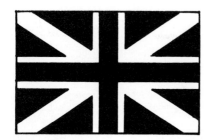

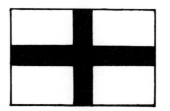

12 WILLIAM SHAKESPEARE

The year he wrote Romeo and Juliet.

You need Sequencing cards M-P to help you with these activities.

1   Look at cards M-P. Put them into chronological order. Then write their numbers in chronological order in these boxes.

☐   ☐   ☐   ☐

2   Look at card M.

   a   Which events happened at the time of this scene?

   b   Why were the fashions so different at that time?

3   Which cards are from these periods?

   a   Tudor

   b   Stuart

   c   Georgian

4   Describe the main developments in:

   a   housing

   b   dress

Using Expansion, trade and industry

Expansion trade and industry is structured as an investigation, focusing on two key questions: 'What changes took place in Britain between 1750 and 1900?' and 'Did these changes make people's lives better or worse?' These questions can be explored and answered at a variety of levels, depending on pupils' ability. The questions are introduced on page 7. Pupils are invited to study the three pictures on pages 4-6, which show life in Britain in the 1750s, 1830s and late 1890s.

Having identified some of the changes which appear to have taken place between 1750 and 1900, pupils are then asked to formulate their first, tentative, hypothesis: 'Did people's lives become better or worse between 1750 and 1900?' This theme is revisited frequently during the book. It is hoped that pupils will become increasingly aware that change does not necessarily mean 'progress', and that the developments which occurred in industrializing Britain had sharply differing effects on people's lives, depending on who they were, and where and when they lived.

Other features of the book are:

a   Opportunities for recording pupils' understanding of Attainment Target elements are signposted by question headings e.g.Changes, Evidence etc. A full list of headings and page numbers of exercises is on page 2 of the book.

b   Each chapter provides a chronological development of the key themes covered in the book. Although the chapters are to a large extent 'self contained', it would seem to make good historical sense to follow the sequence suggested, at least for the first four chapters, which focus on economic change.

c   A Record of Achievement is provided on pages 37-40 of this Resource book which contains key questions from each chapter, and which pupils can use to keep a pupil log of their hypothesis development. This can be photocopied as a double-sided A3 leaflet.

The following chapter by chapter notes may assist planning and show links to material in this Resource book.

Chapter 2 looks at change in the countryside and the effects it had on people's lives. Pages 9 (questions 3 and 4) and 11 offer pupils the chance to evaluate the benefits and defects of key changes. These issues could be addressed through group work or in the form of a class debate. However, they would be equally effective as pieces of individual research. The general focus is on causation and contemporary attitudes.

Chapter 3 investigates the changes that took place in British industry, examining the technological and economic changes, then their effects on people's lives. The dual focus of the chapter allows pupils to extend their understanding of change and of contemporary attitudes. Supporting worksheet Resource book sheet 54.

Chapter 4 investigates the changing nature and extent of British trade between 1750 and 1900. The initial focus is on the growth of empire, and the possible links between expanding empire and expanding trade. The chapter goes on to examine problems with trade – mercantilism, free trade and protection, the questions on page 29 focusing on evidence. The slave trade is dealt with more thoroughly in this Resource book on sheet 42. The final section looks at the benefits of trade, and the questions on page 30 are intended to strengthen an awareness that different groups of people were affected differently: ordinary people actually benefited, in the short-term at least, from cheaper foreign goods by the late nineteenth century! (It may help to be aware that the text on page 29 states that Britain imported more goods than she exported in 1900; Source E on page 26 appears to contradict this. However, the export figures in Source E for 1890-99 include substantial 'invisible' exports, such as financial services.)

Chapter 5 looks at the changes in communications in the period. The chapter first looks at physical communications and their effect on people's lives; it then examines the implications of major non-physical developments such as the post and the telephone. The questions on pages 33 and 37 lend themselves particularly well to small group work. To supplement the chapter pupils could use Resource book sheets 52-3.

Chapter 6 looks at changing living conditions in towns. A grid is used to examine the problems in everyday life created by the growth of towns and to assess the efficiency of the various methods used to solve them. The position of those who were unable to cope is then investigated. Pupils could work individually, or in groups with each group reporting back on a different section. The questions on page 42 allow an investigation of evidence, while causation is addressed on page 45. To supplement the chapter pupils could use Resource book sheets 51 and 55.

Chapter 7 investigates political changes in this period. Some pupils may be unfamiliar with general political concepts, and the introduction aims to provide a brief framework for this. The role of the monarchy today (page 49) might be used as a basis for class discussion. The section on Chartism (pages 54-55) might lead to empathy work, perhaps in the form of a class debate between pro and anti-Chartists. The sections on trade unions, women's rights and Ireland are all useful for highlighting the very slow, patchy effects of change, and the considerable limits to 'progress'. Extension work on A Woman's Place is to be found on sheet 45 of this Resource book.

Chapter 8 brings together leisure, education and religion. The section on leisure involves an investigative approach to a wide range of evidence. It should be possible to identify three broad phases in the development of leisure activities for ordinary people – the disorganized, often brutal nature of leisure in the late eighteenth century; the lack of opportunities for leisure in the mid-nineteenth century; and the growth of organized sports and more technologically advanced leisure activities by the nineteenth century. In the section on religion, the statistical sources (F-H) suggest a decline in church-going by the nineteenth century: this need not necessarily indicate that religion became less important. Question 4 (page 73) aims to develop an awareness that the limited nature of the evidence available makes it impossible to prove that 'a lack of enthusiasm for religion affected all classes'.

Chapter 9 pulls together the main themes of the book by focusing first on the reasons for industrial growth. Question 1 (page 74) is essentially a 'revision' exercise, which might best be done on a whole class discussion basis, or by dividing the class into groups to research different aspects. The central hypothesis is revisited on pages 76-77, and question 2 is structured in such a way as to ensure that pupils become aware of the range of effects changes had during this period. The final two sets of questions are designed to reinforce all Attainment Target elements and to encourage pupils to gain an overview of developments in Britain since the Norman Conquest.

Did people's lives become better or worse, 1750-1900?

Name ....

Class .... Teacher .... Date ....

This booklet will help you keep a Record of Achievement of your progress as you investigate whether people's lives got better or worse between 1750 and 1900. Answer each question when you have completed the relevant chapter in the textbook.

Putting together a hypothesis:

CHAPTER ONE

Page 7. My first hypothesis: Did people's lives become better or worse between 1750 and 1900? Using the pictures on pages 4, 5 and 6, fill in the chart to show how people's lives changed.

	1750	1900
TRANSPORT		
INDUSTRY		
FARMING		
CLOTHING		
FOOD/DIET		
HOUSING		
EDUCATION		
LEISURE		

CHAPTER TWO

Page 12, Question 9: Which of these statements do you agree with? Explain your answer carefully.
Between 1750 and 1900 changes in agriculture made life:

a   better for all farmers, farmworkers and their families

b   worse for all farmers, farmworkers and their families

c   better for some farmers, farmworkers and their families

_____

_____

_____

_____

_____

_____

_____

_____

CHAPTER THREE

Page 21, Question 5. Write your own account answering the question 'Did nineteenth-century working conditions get better or worse?'

_____

_____

_____

_____

_____

_____

_____

_____

CHAPTER FOUR

Page 30, Question 5. 'Everyone in Britain benefited from the expansion of trade.' How far do you agree with this statement?

_____

_____

_____

_____

_____

_____

_____

_____

CHAPTER FIVE

Page 38, Question 4. Think back across all the changes in transport and communications in this chapter. Did they make people's lives better or worse?

_____

_____

_____

_____

_____

CHAPTER SIX

page 39.

Changing living conditions, 1750–1900

	Better	The same	Worse
Food/clothes/household goods			
Housing			
Health			
Crime/law and order			
The jobless			

CHAPTER SEVEN

Did the political changes which took place between 1750 and 1900 help to improve people's lives? Try to mention the following:

a parliamentary reform   **b** chartism   **c** trade unions   **d** the position of women   **e** the Irish

CHAPTER EIGHT

Page 67 Question 4. Do the sources provide enough evidence to prove that changes in leisure activities benefited everyboody between 1750 and 1900?

_____

_____

_____

_____

_____

Page 69 Question 6 Do you think that people were better educated by 1900 than they had been in 1750?

_____

_____

_____

_____

_____

_____

_____

_____

Page 73 Question 3 Do you think religion played a part in improving people's lives between 1750 and 1900?

_____

_____

_____

_____

_____

_____

_____

_____

CHAPTER 9 Completing your hypothesis

Look back at your original hypothesis, and think about what you have studied so far. Which of the following statements would you agree with most?

- Life improved for everybody in Britain between 1750 and 1900.
- Life improved for most people in Britain between 1750 and 1900.
- Life improved for a few people in Britain between 1750 and 1900.
- Life got worse for most people in Britain between 1750 and 1900.

_____

_____

_____

_____

_____

_____

_____

Here is a list of sources that historians might use to find out about life in the past:

- parliamentary records
- photographs
- cartoons
- television interviews
- autobiographies
- statistics
- history text-books
- tape-recordings

- parish registers
- buildings
- cave paintings
- letters and diaries
- maps
- videos
- poems and novels
- newspapers

1   Tick the sources that tell us about life in Britain between 1750 and 1900.

2   From the sources you have ticked, decide whether they are examples of
a   documentary
b   visual
c   archaeological evidence, and fill in the chart below.

DOCUMENTARY	VISUAL	ARCHAEOLOGICAL

3   Choose one kind of source. List the questions you would ask to check if it was a reliable source.

4   Historians have much more evidence available to study Britain between 1750 and 1900 than for earlier periods such as the Middle Ages. Do you think this makes their job easier or more difficult?

The Atlantic slave trade

One reason for Britain becoming wealthier after 1750 was the use of slavery. African slaves had been shipped across the Atlantic to the West Indies and America by Europeans since 1513. Britain dominated the slave trade. Liverpool and Bristol were the leading slaving ports.

The Atlantic slave trade was part of a three-way traffic called 'the triangular trade'. Goods made in Europe were exchanged for slaves on the west coast of Africa. These slaves were usually prisoners of war, captured in local wars by other African tribes. In the 'Middle Passage', slaves were shipped to be sold to plantation owners in the Americas. Slave labour was then used to produce cotton, sugar and tobacco which was carried back to Europe.

The 'Middle Passage' journey usually took about two months. Slaves were tightly packed on ships in suffocating conditions. Many died from disease. On arrival in the colonies, they were usually auctioned. Prices averaged between £25 and £60. Most slaves were then employed in cultivating crops; others became household servants. Living and working conditions were usually poor and cruel punishments were used. Slaves who rebelled against their conditions could be tortured, hanged or burnt alive.

The first people in Britain who began to actively oppose the slave trade were members of a religious group called the Quakers. In 1787, a Committee for the Abolition of the Slave Trade was set up, and began to collect evidence to show how cruel and degrading the slave trade was. William Wilberforce, a Yorkshire MP, dedicated his life to the abolition of the slave trade, and helped persuade Parliament to make it illegal in 1807. Merchants and plantation owners feared that abolition would ruin their trade and prosperity, and their opposition meant that slavery itself was not abolished in the British Empire until 1833.

Why did slavery last so long?

1   Using the introduction above, and Sources A-C, write a description of the conditions on board a slave ship.

2   Study Sources D and E. What arguments do the writers use against slavery and the slave trade?

3   Study Sources G and H. What arguments do the writers use to justify the continuation of slavery and the slave trade?

4   Study the dates of the sources carefully. Was it possible that, by the 1790s, British people could have known nothing about what conditions on the slave ships were actually like?

5   The slave trade was abolished in 1807, but slavery itself continued in the British Empire until 1833. From what you have read, can you suggest any reasons why slavery lasted so long?

Source A

The first object I saw when I arrived on the coast was the sea, and a slave ship waiting for its cargo. These filled me with astonishment, which was soon converted into terror when I was carried on board. I was soon put down under the decks. With the loathsomeness of the stench, and crying together, I became so sick and low that I was not able to hear, nor had I the least desire to taste any thing. I now wished for the last friend, death, to relieve me; but soon, to my grief, two of the white men offered me eatables; and, on my refusing to eat, one of them held me fast by the hands, and tied my feet, while the other flogged me severely.

(Olaudah Equiano was taken from the ancient West African kingdom of Benin to Barbados. Eventually freed, he became active in the British anti-slavery campaign, and his memoirs were published in 1789)

Source B

The deck, that is the floor of their rooms, was so covered with the blood and mucous which had proceeded from them in consequence of the flux, that it resembled a slaughter-house. It is not in the power of human imagination to picture to itself a situation more dreadful or disgusting.

(Alexander Falconbridge, a slave ship surgeon, writing in 1788, describes conditions at sea)

Source C

A plan of a slave ship.
(Plans like these were used in the late eighteenth century as part of the campaign to expose the evils of the slave trade)

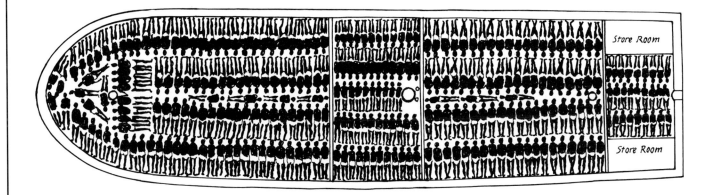

Source D

By incessant labour, the continual application of the lash, and the most inhuman treatment that imagination can devise, you overwhelm the genius of the African and hinder it from breaking forth. The unfortunate Africans have no hope of riches, power, honours, fame. They have no hope but this, that their miseries will be soon terminated by death. The wretched Africans are torn from their country for as long as slavery continues.

(Thomas Clarkson, a leading abolitionist, writing in 1786)

Source E

I would to God it may never be found more: that we may never more steal and sell our brethren like beasts; never murder them by thousands. It cannot be, that either war, or contract, can give any man such a property in another as he has in his sheep and oxen. Much less is it possible, that any child of man should ever be born a slave. Liberty is the right of every human creature.

(John Wesley, in *Thoughts on Slavery*, 1788)

Source F

Instruments of control

Source G

If abolition shall take place, our interest in the West-India islands must be at an end. Seventy millions of property will wear away with time, and be sunk at last. The revenue will suffer an annual reduction of three millions at least; the price of sugar, which is now become a necessary article of life, must be immediately increased.

(William Beckford, in *A Descriptive Account of the Island of Jamaica,* 1790)

Source H

We know, and are ready to prove, that the general condition of the Slaves has been most grossly misrepresented by the London Anti-Slavery Society. We are convinced that the 'speedy annihilation' of Slavery would result in the devastation of the West India Colonies, with the loss of lives and property to the White Inhabitants, with inevitable distress and misery to the Black Population, and with a fatal shock to the commercial credit of this Empire.

(In Defence of Slavery, taken from a pro-slavery broadsheet, 1831)

A woman's place

By the late nineteenth century, women had gained a number of important legal rights, but had still not been given the right to vote in elections to Parliament. Many men – and women – were still opposed to the idea of women's 'suffrage'. It was commonly believed that women were not capable of taking part in what were regarded as men's activities. Study the following sources carefully. Each of them indicates commonly held attitudes towards men and women's traditional roles. For each of the following explain your answer carefully.

1   Study the Sources below. Which of the Sources suggest that:

a   women were not thought capable of becoming judges or lawyers?

b   women were not as intelligent as men?

c   women had a duty to obey men?

d   women who were not interested in family life were worthless?

e   women would be incapable of running the country properly?

2   Study Source A. What types of activity did Tennyson think that

a   men and

b   women should be involved in?

3   Study Sources B and D. What do both writers agree should be women's main aim in life?

4   Study Source C. How does the cartoonist suggest that:

a   women would not make good soldiers or sailors?

b   women would not make good scientists?

c   it would not be right for men to take over women's traditional responsibilities?

5   Source A is from a poem; Source C is a cartoon; Source D is from a novel. Does this mean that the evidence in them is unreliable, and should not be trusted by historians? Explain your answer.

Source A

Man for the field and woman for the hearth;
Man for the sword and for the needle she;
Man with the head and woman with the heart;
Man to command and woman to obey;
All else confusion.

(Alfred Lord Tennyson, *The Princess*, 1847)

Source B

Ever since the world was created, the great mass of women have been of weaker mental power than men and with an instinctive tendency to submit themselves to the control of the stronger sex. Their destiny is marriage, their chief function is maternity, their sphere is domestic and social life.

(*The Times*, 21 May 1867, following a proposal by J. Stuart Mill, MP, that women should be given the vote)

Source C

'Woman's Rights 1981 and What Came of It'. A late nineteenth-century cartoon 'satirising' women's ambitions, and predicting what would happen if they were all achieved.

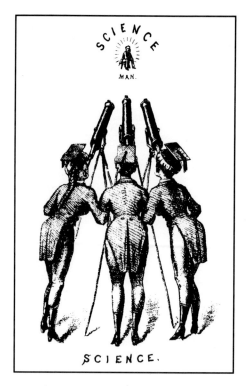

Source D

Wherever you look now-a-days there's sham and rottenness; but the most worthless creature living is one of these trashy, flashy girls, the kind of girl you see everywhere, high and low, calling themselves 'ladies', thinking themselves too good for any honest, womanly work. Town and country, it's all the same. They're educated; oh yes, they're educated! What sort of wives do you think they'd make, with their education? What sort of mothers are they? Before long, there'll be no such thing as a home. They don't know what the word means. They'd like to live in hotels, and trollop about the streets day and night. It is astounding to me that they don't get their necks wrung.

(George Gissing, *In the Year of Jubilee*, 1894)

You need Sequencing cards 13-24 to help you with these activities.

1   Cut out and stick the pictures into your book, or onto paper, in chronological order. You may need to use the textbook, or other reference books to help you.

2   Which pictures shows an event that occurred after 1900?

3   Some pictures show an event that can be precisely dated. For example, the Peterloo Massacre took place on Monday 16 August 1819. Which other pictures show an event that can be precisely dated?

4   Which pictures would be of most use to:

a   a military historian?

b   a political historian?

c   an economic historian?

d   a social historian?

5   Which events shown in the pictures do you think were the most important in the history of Britain during this period? Choose three, and explain the reasons for your choice.

6   Which event shown in the pictures do you think was the least important in the history of Britain during this period? Explain the reasons for your choice.

13   An early telephone exchange

14   The opening of the Liverpool and Manchester Railway

15   The execution of Louis XVI during the French Revolution

16   A Boulton and Watt rotative steam engine

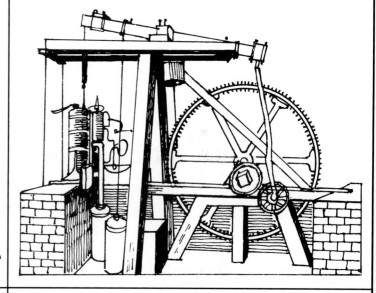

17   Florence Nightingale nursing in Scutari during the Crimean War

18   The death of Nelson at the Battle of Trafalgar

19 The Peterloo Massacre – soldiers cut their way through the crowd

20 The Crystal Palace – home of the Great Exhibition

21 Demonstrators protesting against the transportation of the Tolpuddle martyrs'

22 Soldiers go 'over the top' in the First World War

23 A scene from the Battle of Waterloo

24 A view of Cromford – the first modern factory

This sheet will help you decide if life in the countryside got better or worse between 1750 and 1900.

Read the table below of the main changes in the countryside between 1750 and 1900 and answer the following questions.

Changes in the countryside 1750-1900

Enclosures

The land was enclosed into separate fields owned by individual farmers. Rich farmers bought up the land of those who could not afford enclosure and large farms were created. Farmers therefore had the space and money to try new ideas.

Marl, manure, and new fertilizers

These improved the soil and made it produce more crops per acre.

Selective breeding

Farmers separated the best animals from herds and bred them to produce even better animals.

New machines

People developed new iron machinery. Later steam-powered machines were also used for some jobs.

Four-field rotation

New crop rotations using turnips and ray grass were developed. This restored the goodness of the soil without the need for a fallow field. It meant that turnips and ray grass could be used as cattle fodder and there was no need to slaughter the animals you could not feed in winter.

Transport

Roads and canals made it easier to move agricultural goods to market. They also helped ideas spread because people travelled more and the postal service improved.

Banks

The development of banks provided a way for farmers to borrow money to improve their farms.

Larger farms and long leases

Larger farms meant that improvements were easier to make. Landlords were also willing to grant longer leases to farmers who were keen to try out new ideas. This led to further improvements

Drainage

Land was often too wet for crops to grow. Improved drainage using ditches and clay pipes led to higher yields of crops as existing land was made less boggy and new land was developed.

Wages

In 1882 a commission on the state of agriculture found that the wages of full-time farmworkers had risen so that the average wage bill of some farms was at least 25% higher than it had been in the 1850s. Food and household goods had been cheap and plentiful, while cuts in wages had only occurred in a few areas. However, many farmers were making greater use of temporary gang workers. The gang workers, who were often women and children had to work very long hours for low wages.

Model farms and festivals

New ideas were spread using model farms and festivals.

Employment

Employment in the countryside also changed between 1750 and 1900.

a Total number of farmworkers
1850 male 1,124,000 female 143,000
1907 male 674,000 female 13,500

b Percentage of the population living in urban and rural areas.

	Urban	Rural
1700	20	80
1811	37	63
1901	77	23

1 List the three most important changes in the period. Give the reasons for your choice.
2 Do you think a poor farmworker living in the period would agree with you? Explain your answer.
3 Which of the changes in agriculture between 1750 and 1900 still affect our lives today?
4 Would you rather have lived in the countryside in 1750 or 1900?

Living conditions in towns – A summary

This sheet will help you decide if life in towns got better or worse between 1750 and 1900.

Use the table below to answer the following questions.

1   Which do you think were the three most important developments in living conditions between 1750 and 1900?

2   Which problems existed between 1750 and 1900 which still exist today?

3   Did life get better or worse between 1750 and 1900? Explain your answer.

4   Would you have rather lived in
   a   the Middle Ages
   b   the period 1500-1750 or
   c   the period 1750-1900?
   Explain your answer.

Living conditions in towns, 1750-1900

Diet	Clothing	Housing	Health
New transport methods meant that fresh food became more readily available and there was a greater choice of food. But, in 1900 a third of the population still could not afford an adequate diet.	Mass production made clothes more readily available and increased the choice of clothes for the less well off, but in 1900 a third of the population still could not afford adequate clothing.	After 1875 **a** Local councils were given the power to clear slums. **b** New houses had to have walls of a good thickness, piped water, toilets and damp proofing. But in 1900 a third of the population still could not afford adequate housing. Throughout the period the better-off lived in large villas with servants, but by 1900 good servants were becoming harder to find.	After 1848 various Public Health Acts made it possible for local areas to insist that new houses had drains and toilets, to force people to have piped water in their homes, and to charge a rate to pay for improvements. Local governments also had to lay sewers and drains, and build reservoirs, swimming baths, parks and public toilets. Even so, in 1900 a third of the population still lived in areas with inadequate public health.
Medicine	**Crime**	**The very poor**	
There was a great development in the skill of doctors and in standards of nursing. Diseases like smallpox were controlled by vaccination. Innoculations also began; these stopped the threat of the great killer diseases such as cholera and typhoid. But in 1900 medical attention was still often only available to the rich.	A new police force and harsh prison sentences were used to deal with the growing problem of crime in the cities.	The unemployed, homeless and elderly often had no option but to enter a workhouse; these were made deliberately harsh. In 1900 there were still no old age pensions or unemployment benefit paid by the government.	

Communications timeline

This sheet will help you decide how communications changed between 1750 and 1900.

Look at the pictures and list of dates below.

1   Match the events in the pictures to the correct gaps on the list.
2   Rearrange the list of dates into order and draw a time line to illustrate the changes in communications between 1750 and 1900.
3   List the five most significant developments. Give the reasons for your decision.
4   What developments in communications have occurred since 1900? How have they affected people's lives?

Major changes in communications 1750-1900

1750	Journey time from London to Edinburgh by road – 10 days
1750-1791	1,600 new turnpikes set up
1791-1830	2,450 new turnpikes set up
1765	Blind Jack Metcalfe builds his first road
1784	
1803-1821	Telford builds 1,000 miles of road
1815	Macadam's new road-building methods spread rapidly after this date
1830	Journey time from London to Edinburgh by road – 2days
1759	Duke of Bridgewater employs Brindley to build the Bridgewater Canal
1766	
1830	4,000 miles of canal completed
1802	Trevithick develops the high-pressure steam engine
1825	The Stockton to Darlington Railway opens
1829	
1830	Liverpool to Manchester Railway opens
1840	1,857 miles of railway now complete
1844-1846	438 new railways built
1855	8,000 miles of railway now complete
1870	15,557 miles of railway now complete
1850	Railways begin to carry more freight than canals
1837	Telegraph invented
1840	'Penny post' introduced by Rowland Hill
1850	Telegraph cable laid across the English Channel
1866	Telegraph cable laid across the Atlantic
1876	Telephone invented by Alexander Graham Bell
1884	
1885	Benz drives a car with a petrol engine
1885	Safety bicycle invented
1885	Trams were first electrified
1888	Pneumatic tyre invented by John Dunlop
1894	The steam turbine first used to power ships – this allowed much greater speeds
1896	Daily Mail launched

Picture One

Trent-Mersey Canal built and canals grow rapidly in popularity

Picture Two

Daimler drives a motor cycle with a petrol engine

Picture Three

Palmer begins his Mail Coaching Service between London and Bristol

Picture Four

Stephenson's 'Rocket' wins the Rainhill Trial

Would you make a good factory boss?

In the early nineteenth century people disagreed over the best way to organize the new factories. There were few government regulations. The factory owners had to decide on which method they thought best. Different factory bosses used all the possible approaches set out below.

Each of the approaches has benefits and defects. If you owned a factory which would you choose? Explain your answer.

1 Would you employ?
   a only men?
   b women and men?
   c men, women, and children?

Do not forget it was felt to be quite normal for children to work. In fact they were a vital part of family income: many families could not survive without them working. Children were cheaper than adults and could do tasks men and women could not do. Women were usually paid less than men. Do not forget you need people to run the factory as well as work in it.

2 Would you make them work
   a the longest possible hours?
   b short hours with reasonable breaks?

3 Would you use harsh punishments e.g., fines for lateness, beatings for misbehaviour, beatings to keep your workers awake?

4 Would you be willing to spend money to improve the safety of your factory?

5 Would you treat your employees well e.g., build houses for them, set up a hospital for them, look after them in retirement?

6 How would you react if the employees tried to set up a trade union?

Trade unions were groups of workers who joined together to improve their working conditions. Some employers sacked workers who joined unions, some made their workers sign agreements not to join a union, others negotiated with the unions.

7 Demand for your product falls. Would you
   a lower the price of your product and accept a fall in profits?
   b sack workers and make less goods?
   c cut the price of your product and cut your workers' wages?

8 The price of your raw materials rises. Would you
   a keep the price of your product the same and accept a fall in profits?
   b keep the price of your product the same and cut your workers' wages?
   c put your prices up, produce less and sack some workers?

Prison conditions

In the early nineteenth century people began to criticize the conditions in British prisons.

Read the sources below and answer the questions.

1 What do these sources tell us about conditions in early nineteenth-century prisons?
2 What would you need to know about the sources before you could judge their reliability?
3 Read the information about Elizabeth Fry. How would this effect your view of her source?
4 If the sources were biased, would this make them less valuable to a historian?
5 a What other types of sources would you want to obtain before you could make a full judgement of nineteenth-century prison conditions?
   b Why might some of these be very difficult to obtain?

Source A

The debtors' gaol is divided into two divisions, the Masters' side and the Common side. The Masters' side is for those who can afford to pay for their comforts; the Common side is for those debtors who can afford to pay little or nothing. The rooms on the Masters' side are kept empty, some with but one or two persons in them. On the Common side, most of the rooms contain up to 50 persons locked in a room 16 feet square. The air is so wasted by the number of people who breathe in that narrow space that several prisoners have stifled in the Summer for want of air. The stench is disgusting. All they get to eat is an occasional allowance of peas and beef.

(House of Commons journals, 1729. Conditions like these remained until 1823.)

Source B

In visiting prisons I was sorry to see children so exposed to the wickedness of certain women. The first words the children spoke were swear words. Women who came to prison weeping over their crimes would be laughing and joking by the time of their trial. They seem to have been trained for almost any crime whilst in prison. It therefore struck me that it was important to separate women and children from the hardened criminals.

(Elizabeth Fry, writing in the early nineteenth century.)

Information: Elizabeth Fry 1780-1845

Elizabeth Fry was a Quaker from a wealthy family. In 1813 she was asked to visit the women in Newgate Prison. She was disgusted by the conditions and began to campaign for reform. She called for changes in the way women and children were kept. She tried to teach the prisoners' children and to spread the Christian message. Her ideas influenced the prison reforms of Robert Peel.

In the period 1750-1900 mass production and changes in transport led to the development of shops and the rapid growth of advertising.

To find out more you must investigate the sources below.

Before you start

1   make a list of the questions you would want to ask about shops and advertising.

As you investigate the sources decide

2   what problems are there in finding answers to your questions.

At the end consider

3   which questions were easiest to answer and why?
4   which questions were hardest to answer and why?
5   why might historians have different answers to some questions?

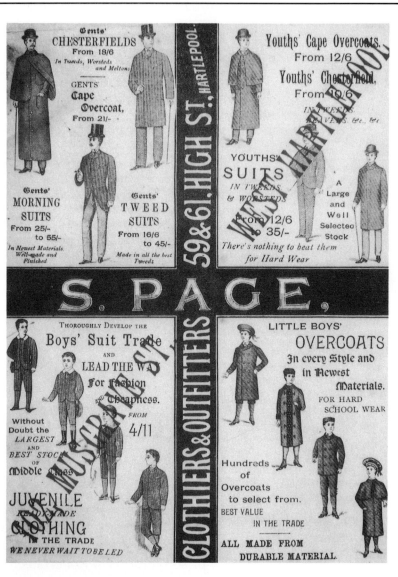

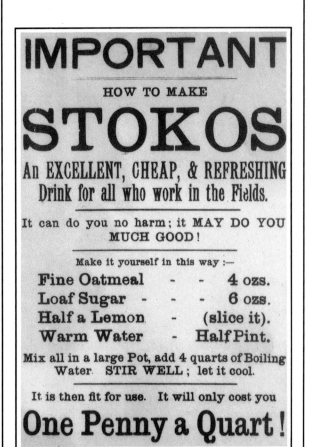

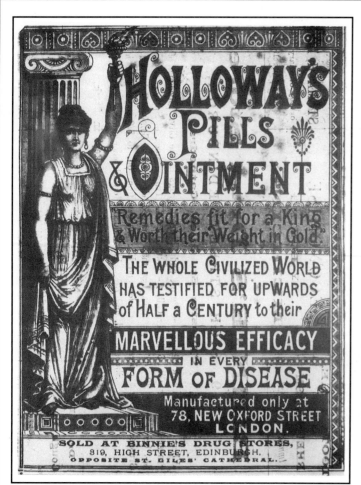

Using Britain and the Great War

Britain and the Great War is structured along the same investigative lines as the other books in the series. The two key questions of this book are: 'Why did the First World War last so long?' and 'How did it change Britain?' For both these questions pupils are provided with some initial sources from which they are invited to formulate an hypothesis in answer to each of these questions.

These hypotheses are recorded on the hypothesis grid on pages 6 and 30. As they make their way through the text they will discover material which either supports or refutes their original hypothesis. They should make a note of this evidence on their grids. They may discover that their original ideas were wrong but this should not be seen as a mistake but merely as an example of the historical process at work: all historical judgements are provisional and contingent on the available evidence.

Less able pupils may encounter some problems with formulating their own hypotheses from the evidence. More structured support from the teacher would be beneficial here.

Chapter 1 is concerned with the causes of the war. The first grid-based exercise attempts to get across the distinction between long and short term causes, and economic, and political causes. It concludes by introducing the notion of a hierarchy of causation by asking the pupils to identify what they consider to be the most important cause of the war. There is no particular correct answer here – the only criterion is the way evidence is deployed in support of the argument. There is a resource sheet in this book on the relative strengths of the powers in 1914 (sheet 60).

Chapter 2 deals with life in the trenches and the war on other fronts. The source-based exercise on page 13 focuses on the different attitudes to the war prevalent among the troops and the dangers inherent in the partial selection of evidence. This and chapters 3 and 4 all provide useful material for the hypothesis grid. There are sheets in this resource book which look at the casualty rate among officers and men (sheet 67), why casualties were so high (sheet 68), why some men were keen to fight (sheet 65), and why others later became disillusioned (sheet 69).

The exercise on Jutland gets across to pupils the idea that observers at the time are often ill-placed to assess the significance of an event – in this case the Battle of Jutland. At the time, the battle could justly be seen as a German victory but in retrospect it was clearly a strategic British victory – a fact which historians later would be able to appreciate. In class use pupils have answered question 3 from both points of view ie that the decision of Jellicoe was both more/less understandable. Both can be argued. There is a resource sheet exercise on the effectiveness of anti-U-boat measures (sheet 70).

Chapter 3 attempts to develop the notion of change and continuity in military technology and strategy by comparing 1815 with 1914. The strategy had not changed but the technology was now more destructive – a recipe for the slaughter. The value of the tank is the focus of a source-based exercise on page 23 and one which looks at contrasting assessments – both primary and secondary. There are resource sheet exercises on why it was so difficult to launch surprise attacks (sheet 62) and why so many offensives failed (sheet 63).

Chapter 4 deals with the variety of motives which men had for volunteering for the war: motives of patriotism, honour, adventure, peer group pressure, fear of ostracism, poverty. The emphasis is on differentiated responses both in terms of those opting for war and those who opposed it. The element of disillusion which began to spread – especially after 1916 – is reflected in several of the sources on page 29. There is a resource sheet activity on why some men refused to fight 9 (sheet 69).

Chapter 5 onwards deals with the second of the key questions: how did the war change Britain? The focus of this chapter is on the growth of the power of government evidenced by policies towards conscription, industry, and rationing.

Chapter 6 concludes with one of the most significant social changes brought about by the war: the partial emancipation of women. However, the exercise on page 43 attempts to get pupils to think about the issue of change in its wider context by pointing out that, in some respects at least, not much had changed for women by the time the Second World War broke out. There is a resource sheet activity on how the war affected women (sheet 72).

How did the sides line up in 1914?

The map and statistics which come with this exercise provide an idea of the military and industrial strengths of the European powers in 1914. Complete each of the following tasks on the map and keep it, when completed, in your file or exercise book.

1   First shade in or colour who was on which side. The Entente or Allies in 1914 consisted of Britain, France, Russia, and Serbia. Shade these on your map. Find a similar style to identify those countries which joined the Allies after the war started. These are Italy (who joined in 1915), Romania (1916), Greece (1917), and the USA (1917).

2   The Central Powers consisted of Germany and Austria-Hungary. They were joined by Turkey (1914), and Bulgaria (1915). Shade these on your map.

3   Now fill in the information boxes which you can see on or near each of the following countries on your map. Use the information below.

Country	Peace-time army	Battleships	Steel production
Britain	700,000	64	6.5m tonnes
France	1,250,000	28	3.5m tonnes
Russia	1,300,000	16	4m tonnes
USA	150,000	37	32m tonnes
Italy	750,000	14	–
Germany	2,200,000	40	14m tonnes
Austria-Hungary	800,000	16	3m tonnes
Turkey	360,000	–	–
Bulgaria	340,000	–	–

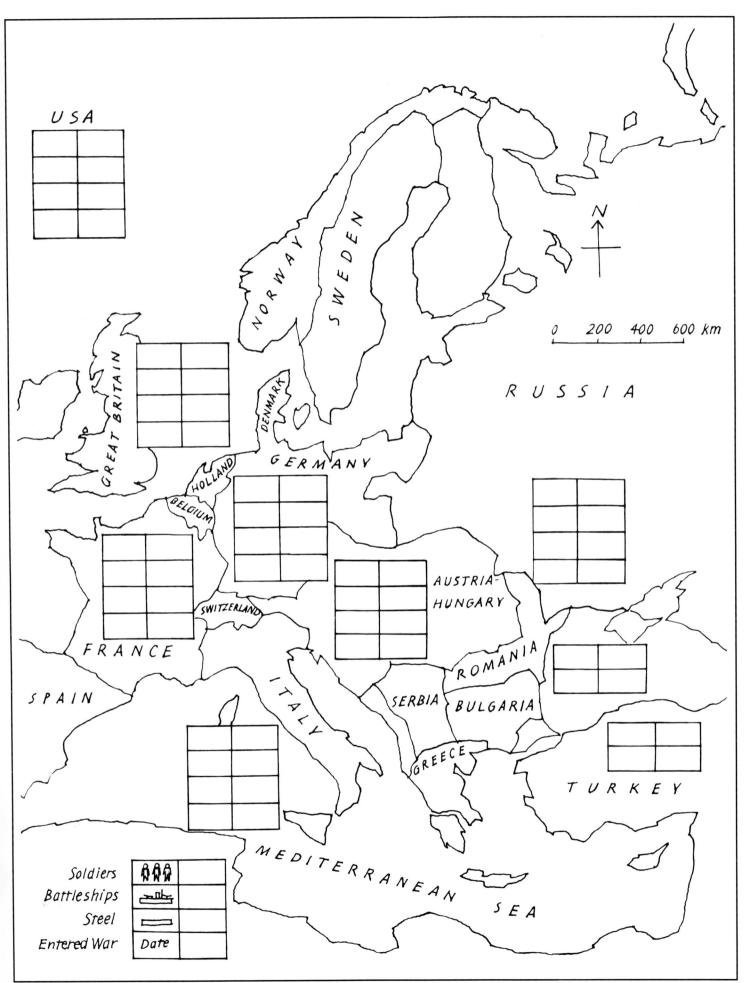

USA

GREAT BRITAIN

NORWAY

SWEDEN

RUSSIA

0   200   400   600 km

DENMARK

GERMANY

HOLLAND

BELGIUM

FRANCE

SWITZERLAND

AUSTRIA-HUNGARY

ROMANIA

SERBIA   BULGARIA

SPAIN

ITALY

GREECE

TURKEY

MEDITERRANEAN SEA

Soldiers	👤👤👤	
Battleships	🚢	
Steel	▭	
Entered War	Date	

Why was it so difficult to launch surprise attacks?

A First World War offensive (attack) took a great deal of planning. The generals had to make many decisions to get the attack to go as smoothly as possible. But often, each decision would have a drawback and this made sure planning was never easy. In this exercise there is a chart which sets out some of the elements of a plan for a big offensive. Each element of the plan has its good points and its drawbacks. Your task is to read the good and bad points and fill in the 'Your Decision' column with your reason.

PLAN	IN FAVOUR	AGAINST	YOUR DECISION
Should mass graves be dug for the dead before the battle?	If the dead are buried quickly there is less risk of disease.	The sight of the graves will be bad for morale; the enemy will get suspicious.	
Should you stockpile huge amounts of ammunition and food as close to the front as possible?	This will mean the troops have enough supplies to hold out against any counter-attack by the enemy.	The enemy will spot the stockpiles and suspect an attack is planned.	
Should you cut a pathway through your own barbed wire the night before for your troops to get through?	Your troops won't get tangled up in your own barbed wire as they go 'over the top'	The enemy might catch your men cutting the wire and find out about the attack.	
Should you order a long 24 hour artillery barrage of the enemy trenches?	The enemy trenches will be severely damaged and some men killed.	The enemy may be able to bring up reinforcements once they realise an attack is planned.	
Should you order a short 2 hour barrage?	The enemy won't have a chance to bring up reinforcements.	A short barrage may not do much damage and some sections of trench won't be hit at all.	
Should you bring in extra troops from the reserve lines to help in the attack?	The attack has a better chance of success if there are more troops involved.	These troops will be spotted by enemy planes making their way to the front: there will be no surprise.	

The illustration on the next page shows a fairly typical infantry attack on well defended enemy trenches. Below are seven reasons which help to explain why attacks so often failed to break through the enemy lines.

Your Task:

1   Each of the seven reasons below contains details which go in the empty boxes on the illustration on the next page. For example, the details about the role of aircraft in a battle should go in the empty box pointing at the plane.

2   Choose three of the reasons now on your illustration which you think are the most important in defeating attacking troops. Explain why each of these reasons helped to defeat enemy attacks.

Zigzagged trenches:

These were protected by sandbags and were 2 metres deep so troops could fire from them without risking being shot at.

Barbed wire:

This was often 10 metres deep and soldiers could only get through it if their own artillery had destroyed it before the attack. (This did not always happen).

Aircraft:

Used as observers to spot troops gathering for an offensive. This made surprise attacks difficult to launch.

Artillery:

These were sited 10 kms behind the lines and fired barrages of shells at attacking troops and their trenches.

Dug outs:

Some of these were up to 15 metres below ground and could resist even direct hits from artillery shells. So, troops were safe in these.

Concrete blockhouses:

These could resist some artillery shells and all machine gun and rifle fire. They contained machine guns firing up to 10 bullets a second.

Shell craters:

These were caused by the explosions of both sides and they slowed down the speed of attacking troops (though they could provide cover as well).

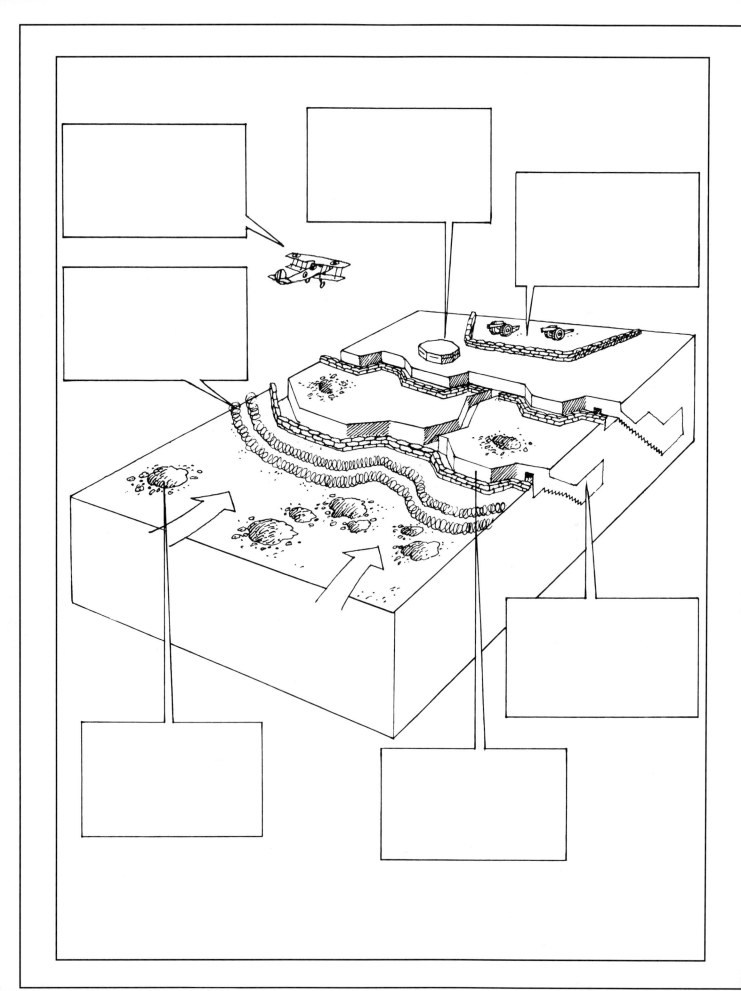

Why did men enlist?

Britain did not introduce conscription until 1916. Up until then all her soldiers were volunteers so they had in common that they wanted to enlist. However, the reasons for wanting to fight were very different as these sources show.

Source A

Harry Parry was a student at Oxford and wrote to his mother explaining why he was going to enlist in the army:

'I have no wish to remain a civilian any longer; and, though the idea of war is against my conscience, I feel that in a time of national crisis like the present, I don't have the right to my views if they are against the best interests of the country'.

Adapted from *Eye Deep in Hell*, J Ellis, 1976

Source B

J Norton, like many other lads, was below the minimum age of nineteen but recruiting sergeants were keen to sign them up because they got a bonus for every man they enlisted in the army:

'I was a member of the village cricket and football teams and nearly every one of their members enlisted. I was only sixteen but I tried to join up, too. The recruiting sergeant asked me my age and when I told him he said, 'You'd better go out, come in again, and tell me different'. I came back, told him I was nineteen and I was in'.

Quoted in *The First Day on the Somme*, M Middlebrook, 1971

Source C

H Fellows joined the Northumberland Fusiliers for this reason:

'Both my parents were dead, I was very poor and had never had a holiday in my life. When I joined up at Nottingham, I refused the local units and... chose the Northumberland Fusiliers because it gave me the longest train ride.'

Quoted in *The First Day on the Somme*, M Middlebrook, 1971

Source D

Another reason for joining was given by WHA Groom:

'A military band and marching soldiers are always an inspiring sight, but this was for real – they were off to war and how we youngsters envied them... And to tell you the truth that was it – glamour – to be in uniform – to take part in a great adventure was as much a reason for so many youths joining up as any sense of patriotism'.

From *Poor Bloody Infantry* W H A Groom

The sources above can be divided into four categories:

A Those who joined up because their friends did (this is called 'peer group pressure')

B Those who enlisted to escape from poverty

C Those who joined out of a sense of duty to the country

D Those who enlisted out of a sense of adventure

1 Fill in the chart below by placing the letter of the source in the right-hand column with the evidence from the source which supports your choice.

Reason for Enlistment	Found in Source because...
Peer group pressure	
To escape poverty at home	
Sense of duty	
Sense of adventure	

2 Is it possible to say which reason above might have been the least important in persuading young men to enlist? Give reasons for your answer.

Who suffered the most casualties: officers or other ranks?

British soldiers on the Western Front had to face the possibility of being killed or wounded. The chance of becoming a casualty – someone who is killed or wounded – also depended on whether you were an officer or from 'other ranks' (any rank below that of a lieutenant, such as a private or corporal). Study the statistics below and then answer the questions which follow.

Source A:

British soldiers killed in the First World War

	Percentage of Officers killed	Percentage of Other Ranks killed
Oct. 1914-Sept. 1915	14%	6%
Oct. 1917-Sept. 1918	7%	4%

Source B:

British soldiers wounded

	Percentage of Officers wounded	Percentage of Other Ranks wounded
Oct. 1914-Sept. 1915	24%	17%
Oct. 1917-Sept. 1918	17%	14%

1 Which type of soldier was more likely to be killed or wounded: officers or other ranks? Explain your reason.
2 What reasons can you give for this? (Think about the role of an officer in a battle).
3 Were British troops more likely to be killed or wounded at the beginning of the war or at the end? What evidence do you have for your answer?
4 'Soldiers were more likely to be killed or wounded at the beginning of the war than at the end. This proves that the fighting at the beginning of the war was more fierce'. Explain why you agree or disagree with this view.

Why were casualties so high?

There are several reasons which help to explain why the First World War led to such heavy casualties. In the chart below is a list of reasons which helped to cause the deaths of so many men. What the chart doesn't do is explain why they led to these deaths.

1   Your task is to fill in the column with why you think these reasons led to so many men being killed or wounded. One has already been filled in for you as an example.

Reason for the high casualties	Your explanation
Factories were able to make huge numbers of shells and weapons	
Both sides used conscription to make men fight	
High explosive shells and the machine gun were very deadly weapons	
Large numbers of troops could be moved very quickly by train	
Neither side could really break through the opposing trench system	
The tank was the only really effective weapon of attack and it wasn't used properly until late 1917	
The front line troops and the generals were not properly in touch with each other because of poor communications	Telephone lines were often cut by the effects of battle and so generals were slow to find out when an attack had failed. This meant that they often carried on with attacks which could never succeed.

2   Choose one reason from the list above which you think was the most important and one which you think was the least important in causing so many deaths.

Why did some men turn against the war?

When war broke out in August 1914 there was tremendous support for it. Nearly 800,000 Britons volunteered for the war in the first two months. However, soon this enthusiasm began to fade and many soldiers began to hate the conflict. Why did their views of the war change so sharply?

Source A

One unnamed volunteer wrote these bitter and humorous lines about his feelings three years into the war:

'Because it seemed the thing to do
I joined with other volunteers
But – well, I don't mind telling you
I didn't reckon for three years.
Though we observe the Higher Law
And though we have our quarrel just
Were I permitted to withdraw
You wouldn't see my arse for dust'.

Source B

For Private Chaney the Battle of the Somme was the turning point:

'From now on the veterans, myself included, decided to do no more than was really necessary, following orders, but if possible keeping out of harm's way. I have the feeling that many of the officers felt the same way'.

Quoted in *Eye Deep in Hell*, J Ellis.

Source C

Richard Stumpf served in the German navy during the war. At first, Stumpf was enthusiastic about the war but by as early as 1915 his views were changing, as this entry in his diary makes clear:

'I no longer care if we get to fight or not... our main interest is food, extra rations and shore leave... The men often express the hope that there will be no battle. For whom should they allow themselves to be killed? For the wealthy?... The officers have made no sacrifices at all so far... While we have to live on half rations of bread, in the officers' mess they hold feasts and drinking bouts at which six or seven courses are served'.

Quoted in *The Great War*, R Tames

Source D

A British soldier, Henry Fell, saw a British officer murdered by his own men when they refused to fight any more:

'Our colonel was shot but I daren't mention any names... He turned round and said: "You cowards". He was hit in the back. It was this colonel who gathered all the stragglers up to try and stop the Germans coming on and he was shot in the back. By his own men'

Quoted in *The Great War*, R Tames

1 What reason does Source A give for wanting to get out of the war?
2 Why do you suppose the Battle of the Somme had the effect it did on the men in Source B?
3 What is Richard Stumpf's opinion of his officers? What effect would this have had on morale?
4 Do you think Stumpf would have approved of the actions of the men in Source D? Explain your answer.
5 Stumpf was a German but do you think his views would have been shared by men in other countries' armies as well? Give reasons for your answer.

What was the most successful way of sinking a U-boat?

German submarines (called U-boats) sank a great deal of British merchant ships during the war. At one stage in 1917, Britain came close to running out of food and being starved into surrender but eventually the U-boat threat was beaten. The British navy used several methods of sinking enemy submarines as the statistics below show. (NB: 'Q-ships' were warships designed to look like unarmed merchant vessels. Submarines would often surface and use their deck gun to sink a merchant ship on its own rather than use a valuable torpedo. When the U-boat came up to the surface to sink its easy prey, it found itself under attack instead from the Q-ship's concealed guns).

Method used	Number sunk
1914-1916:	
By patrol vessels	15
Rammed by warship	2
By 'Q-ships'	5
By mines	7
By merchant ships	0
By convoy escorts	0
By accidents	7
By unknown causes	7
1918:	
By patrol vessels	24
Rammed by warships	1
By Q-ships	0
By mines	18
By merchant ships	4
By convoy escorts	10
By accidents	2
By unknown causes	10

1 Use this outline of a bar graph to plot the statistics given here. It has already been started for you. You can use different colours to shade in the columns for 1914–1916 and for 1918.

2 How many U-boats were sunk during the whole war? (The number for 1917 was 63, so add these to those from the rest of the war).

3 Which was the most successful and the least successful method of sinking German submarines?

4 Why do you think ramming sank so few U-boats?

5 Can you suggest why 'Q-ships' were less successful in sinking U-boats in 1918 than they had been at the beginning of the war? (clue: Q-ships needed to trick the submarines)

6 Britain lost 13 million tons of merchant shipping during the war. U-boats sank 11 million of these 13 million tons. Do you think the German U-boat fleet was a success? Give a reason for your answer.

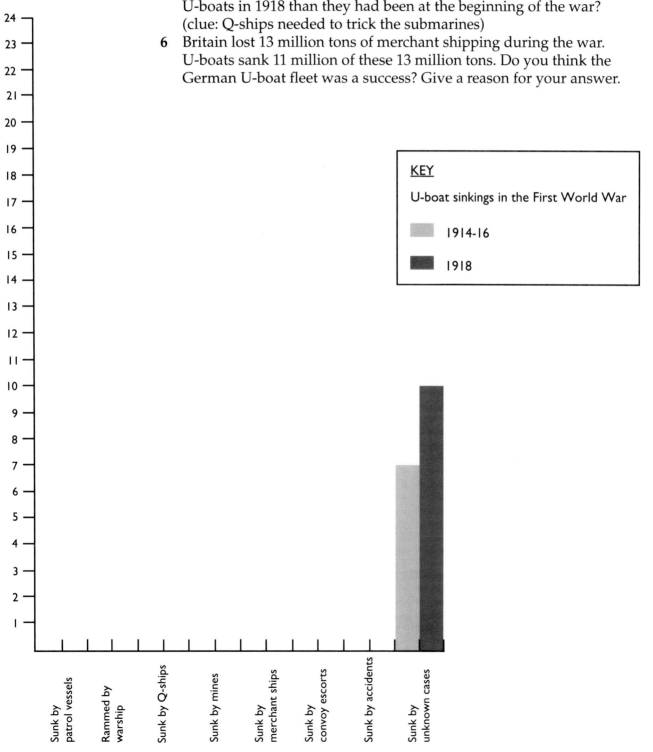

KEY

U-boat sinkings in the First World War

1914-16

1918

What did the war change for women?

To find out whether much changed for women as a result of the war, it's necessary to know what it was like before and after the war. In this way, you have something with which to compare the war-time role of women. It is certainly true that women earned a new respect for the skills they showed in doing 'men's work' during the war. They also experienced new social freedoms. However, did these changes last?

Source A

Women's employment before the First World War

'Domestic service was seen by people as more suitable for young girls than factory work, for example, because women servants were far more 'protected' and 'controlled' than they would be in other kinds of jobs. It was just this lack of independence (along with low pay and long hours) that made domestic work so unpopular, but for many women there was little alternative'.

Women and Work, Patricia Owen, 1989

Source B

Interview with Alfred Shears, a former dock worker:

'...Women didn't go out to work then (before 1914) and it wasn't the thing for women anywhere really. Up in the North they did in the mills, and in London they would go on working, but it was frowned on for a women to work if she was a married women. Single women would be in the shops, but a married woman — her place was in the home'.

Divisions of Labour, R E Pohl, 1984

Source C

War work in the munitions industry

Many women found work during the war making shells (munitions) for the Front. It was dangerous and dirty work but women were still keen to do it: 'I was in domestic work and hated every minute of it when the war broke out, earning £2 a month working from 6.00 am to 9 pm. So when the need came for women 'war workers' my chance came to 'out'. I started on hand cutting shell fuses... We worked twelve hours a day apart from the journey morning and night... As for wages I thought I was very well off earning £5 per week.'

Mrs H A Felstead in a letter to the Imperial War Museum, 1976

Source D

Daisy Noakes — domestic servant after the war

Daisy began her career as a servant at the wage of £14 a year in 1922. She was fourteen:
'My hours were from 5.30 am to 10.30 pm and no let-up anywhere during that time. How I stayed awake I do not know. My off-duty time was Tuesday 2.30 pm to 9.30 pm and one afternoon a fortnight for the same hours... I would not wish a daughter of mine to work as hard as I had to as a child. But it was accepted, because it was the only job for girls, apart from shop assistants'.

from *The Town Beehive – A Young girl's lot*, Daisy Noakes, 1978

Source E

Women's Occupations in the 1911 and 1921 censuses

	1911	1921
Public administration (civil servants, post office workers)	50,000	81,000
Professional occupations (lawyers, doctors, teachers)	383,000	441,000
Domestic service (servants, cooks, maids)	2,127,000	1,845,000
Commercial occupations (clerks, typists)	157,000	587,000

Source F

The first issue of *Women's Own*, 1932

'How do you do?
We introduce ourselves and our new weekly for the modern young wife who loves her home. *Woman's Own* will be a paper with a purpose... The home paper that makes any girl worth her salt want to be the best housewife ever'.

1 In what way do both Sources A and E agree about how common domestic work was for women before the war?
2 Is Source B's claim that women 'didn't go out to work' before the war supported by Sources E and C?
3 Does Source C suggest any reason why munitions work was popular among women – despite the dangers?
4 Is the last sentence of Source D supported by Source E? How can you explain this difference? (Think about the type of job Daisy did and the people she was likely to socialise with).
5 Does Source E suggest that women's career opportunities improved after the war? Give reasons for your answer.
6 Do Sources D and F suggest that attitudes to the role of women changed much after the war?

How was Germany treated by the peace?

Germany surrendered in November 1918 and in June 1919 the Allies presented the Germans with their terms in the Treaty of Versailles. The Germans claimed the terms were both harsh and humiliating but had no option but to sign them. Use the map which comes with this exercise to fill in the details of the treaty and then put it in your file or exercise book.

1 **Territorial losses in Europe** – Germany also lost all of her colonies but these are not shown here. Fill in the boxes on the map with the information provided below in italics:

Alsace–Lorraine: *returned to France*

Saar: *all the coal to go to France for 5 years*

Rhineland: *no German troops or defences here*

North Schleswig: *given to Denmark*

Danzig: *under the control of the League of Nations*

West Prussia: *given to the new state of Poland*

2 **Military terms:**
Army: *limited to 100,000 men*
Tanks: *none allowed*
Aircraft: *no engine powered aircraft*
Battleships: *only 6 allowed*
Submarines: *none allowed*

3 **Reparations**
Germany had to pay £2000 million in compensation to the Allies for the cost of war. This could be paid in gold, coal, timber, and other materials.

4 **Austria**: *forbidden to unite with Germany.*

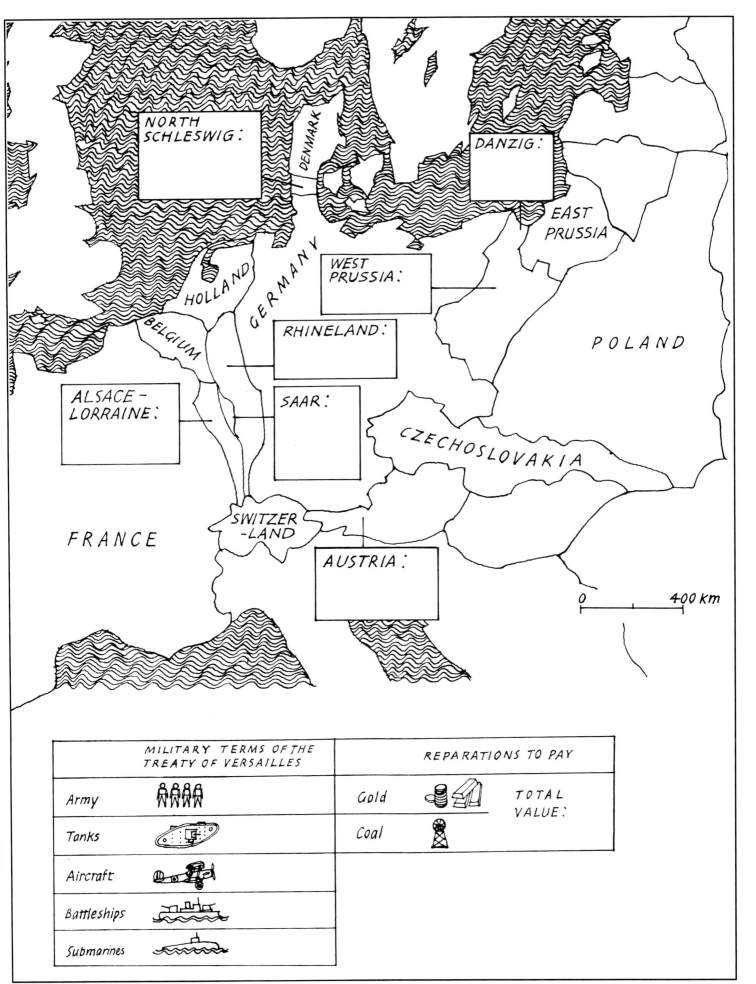

NORTH SCHLESWIG:

DANZIG:

EAST PRUSSIA

DENMARK

HOLLAND

GERMANY

WEST PRUSSIA:

POLAND

BELGIUM

RHINELAND:

ALSACE-LORRAINE:

SAAR:

CZECHOSLOVAKIA

FRANCE

SWITZER-LAND

AUSTRIA:

0   400 km

MILITARY TERMS OF THE TREATY OF VERSAILLES		REPARATIONS TO PAY		
Army		Gold		TOTAL VALUE:
Tanks		Coal		
Aircraft				
Battleships				
Submarines				

Using The era of the Second World War

This book follows the premiss of the others in this series. It is structured as an investigation into the key questions: 'Why did the Second World War not break out before September 1939?' and 'Could the Axis Powers have won the war?' The final section of the book investigates the consequences and impact of the war on Britain and subsequent world history. The idea behind posing these questions and then asking the pupils to formulate their own hypotheses around them is to develop their understanding of the historian's method.

It is expected that their initial hypotheses will be amended as they work through the text and evaluate the new evidence which comes to light. The idea that historical interpretation is always provisional and dependent on the sources available is a cardinal aspect of historical study. An additional motif which runs through the text is that of attempting to demythologize some aspects of how the war has been traditionally perceived in Britain. References are made, for example, to the willingness of some sections of the British establishment to treat with Hitler in 1940. The less vaunted aspects of Dunkirk are related as are the continued industrial tensions and class divisions of Britain at war. The purpose behind this is not to belittle the remarkable achievements of the British people against a despicable foe but to emphasize that the point of history is to get as close to the ungarnished truth as possible.

Introduction

The traditional approach to the outbreak of the war is to ask why war broke out in September 1939. However, pupils often produce their best work when asked to consider a familiar issue in an unfamiliar way. This is the rationale behind the question in the introduction – 'Why did the war not break out before September 1939?'. In answering this question they will inevitably establish why it did break out when it did and avoid the simple answer that it was Hitler's fault.

Chapter 2 looks at the consequences of the First World War and provides pupils with evidence which illustrates the sense of bitterness which was prevalent after the war. It also seeks to compare the Europe of the nineteenth and early twentieth centuries with that of the 1920s and 1930s. The point of this is to encourage pupils to identify the many similarities and differences between the two epochs. The text then moves on to the Europe of the 1920s, highlighting those factors which made a confrontation between the great powers less likely.

Chapter 3 takes up the impact of three major dictatorships – Japan, Italy and Germany – on the balance of world power. The decade of the 1930s is sharply contrasted with that of the 1920s in terms of economic and political stability, encouraging the pupils to explore these factors as contributors to war in 1939. The Resource book contains an exercise on the options facing the British government in March 1939 (sheet 78), and concludes the first question.

Chapter 4 moves onto the second question: 'Could the Axis have won the war?' and asks the pupils to consider a variety of sources relating to the possibility of an Axis victory in the war and then goes on to discuss the war in Europe and North Africa up to 1943. Relevant Resource book activities on this chapter relate to Dunkirk (sheet 82) the Battle of Britain (sheet 85), the bombing of Coventry and the nature of the war at this time (sheet 87). The Dunkirk activity tries to contrast how the evacuation was covered in the press at the time with an uncensored version of the pupils' own devising. The Coventry exercise confronts pupils with the dilemma faced by Churchill who knew in advance of the heavy raid but chose not to warn the population.

Chapter 5 completes the section on the war in Europe, covering the invasion of Russia, the war in Italy, the Normandy landings, the Bomber Offensive over Germany and the Battle of the Atlantic. Issues of particular significance dealt with in the text concern the controversies over the bombing of Monte Cassino and Germany. Relevant Resource book activities include a map exercise on Barbarossa (sheet 91), and a causation activity on why Germany lost the war (sheet 95).

Chapter 6 deals with the war in the Pacific from 1941 to its conclusion. A focal point of this chapter concerns the moral, military and political issues raised by the atomic bombing of Hiroshima and Nagasaki. There is a causation exercise in the Resource book on the bombing of Pearl Harbor (sheet 96) which concludes the second question.

Chapter 7 looks at the impact of the war on the civilian population of Britain and at the Holocaust. A particular focus of this chapter is how the war changed social and political attitudes among the population. There is material relating to continued industrial relations problems and class tensions in general. Many of these issues are explored through the treatment of women and some attempt is made to assess the extent of the changes which affected them. The Holocaust is treated largely via an extensive eye-witness account of a massacre in the Ukraine. A relevant, Resource book activity at this stage is a detective exercise on the massacre at Oradour in France (sheet 97). This last assignment seeks to show how established interpretations of the past may be re-evaluated in the light of new evidence.

Chapter 8 concludes the book with a look at the long-and short-term consequences of the war. Among its themes are the emergence (and demise) of the Cold War, the end of the European order and the post-war role of the United Nations.

Hypothesis grid: Why did war not break out before September 1939?

Possible reasons	Effects	Evidence
The First World War	The First World War caused so many deaths that people would do anything to avoid another war.	
The Treaty of Versailles	The Germans felt unfairly punished by this treaty and wanted to see it torn up.	The Germans resented the cuts in their armed forces – only 100,000 soldiers in their army which was now very weak.
Pro-peace attitudes in Britain		
The attitudes of the world powers to Hitler		
Hitler's secret plan, 1936		
Rearmament in the 1930s		During 1939 Britain and France built more planes than Germany for the first time since 1933. Therefore, they were more ready for war now.
The German invasion of Poland		Hitler's invasion of Poland did lead to the outbreak of war with Britain and France but he was expecting them to fight over Poland.

Czechoslovakia 1939 – choosing war or peace?

In September 1938, German troops occupied a part of Czechoslovakia called the Sudetenland. This had been agreed with Britain, France and Italy – though not Czechoslovakia! Hitler promised that he would make no more demands for land in Europe and it seemed that Europe could look forward to peace and stability. Six months later Hitler suddenly ordered German troops to seize the rest of the country. This clearly broke Hitler's promise of September 1938.

Chamberlain, the British Prime Minister, had to decide what Britain's reaction would be. Your task is to look at the various options open to the government at the time and put together a report with your recommendation for Chamberlain to read. The information below will help you with this.

1 German expansion in Europe, 1936-39

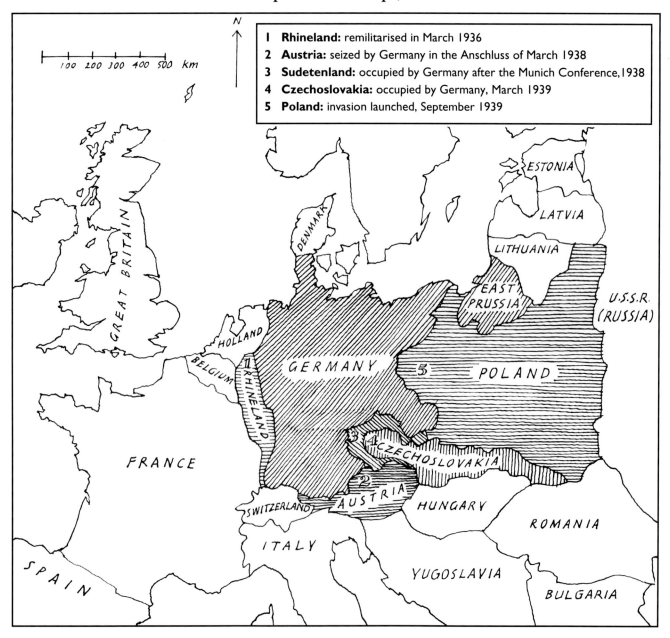

1 **Rhineland:** remilitarised in March 1936
2 **Austria:** seized by Germany in the Anschluss of March 1938
3 **Sudetenland:** occupied by Germany after the Munich Conference, 1938
4 **Czechoslovakia:** occupied by Germany, March 1939
5 **Poland:** invasion launched, September 1939

2 Hitler's record in power

1935 Hitler introduced conscription – a breach of the Treaty of Versailles.

1936 Hitler ordered German troops into the Rhineland area of Germany – also against the Treaty of Versailles.

1938 German troops occupied Austria – another breach of the treaty.

1938 Hitler promised that the Sudetenland was the last piece of territory Germany wanted in Europe.

1939 German troops ordered to seize the rest of Czechoslovakia.

3 British, German and French military strength in 1939

	Soldiers	Aircraft	Major warships
Germany	800,000	2765	11
Britain	220,000	1100	76
France	800,000	735	21

(France was Britain's ally at the time.)

4 Hitler's next step?

Hitler's clear policy since coming to power has been to bring all those Germans living outside Germany under German rule. Austria was occupied because there were 7 million Austrian Germans living there. The Sudetenland was taken over because there were 3 million Germans living there. There are also one million Germans living in Poland. Hitler claims they are being ill-treated by the Polish government.

Your assignment

Write a 300 word report for Chamberlain, giving your assessment of the situation in Europe in late-March 1939 and what the government should do next. It will help you to consider the following points:

1 Can we do anything to help Czechoslovakia now? Is Britain in a position to fight Germany – with or without French help? How easy would it be to get land forces to Czechoslovakia?

2 Is Hitler likely to call a halt now to his programme of expansion? Does his track record suggest he can be trusted?

3 Poland could be his next target. Should Britain offer to defend her if attacked by Germany? Why should we defend Poland (a country run by a dictator) and not Czechoslovakia (a democracy)?

4 Is a war in Europe likely and what should Britain do to prepare for it?

5 Are the British people, so soon after the Great War, prepared to fight another?

You do not have to write your report in five sections and you can, of course, add any other ideas of your own which you think are important.

Germany and the League of Nations in the 1930s

Column A: **Factors explaining German reluctance to challenge the League of Nations in the 1920s**	Column B: **Your view on whether the reasons in Column A were still relevant during the1930s**	Column C: **Evidence from Sources I-N and from what you have read in the text so far which supports your answer in Column B**
Germany did not have a powerful enough military force in the 1920s to try to challenge the terms of the Treaty of Versailles and the authority of the League.		
Germany was a democracy and was prepared to co-operate with Britain and France in keeping to the treaty.		
Germany was prosperous during most of the 1920s and so the Germans were less bothered by memories of the treaty because they were doing well.	Germany was increasingly prosperous after the Depression of 1929-32. The evidence of Sources L and M proves this. The Germans were well off in the late 1930s yet then they defied the League and the treaty so it could not have been very important in the 1920s.	
No other major European power was willing to join with Germany in challenging the treaty and the League during the 1920s.		

Hypothesis grid: Could the Axis powers have won the Second World War?

Possible theories	Evidence in support of /against your hypothesis
The Axis powers (Germany and Italy) could have won the war in 1940.	In the view of The Spectator (Source D), only Britain stood in the way of Germany controlling all of Europe. Therefore, Germany must have been close to victory.
The Axis powers could still have won the war in 1941.	
From 1942 onwards the Axis Powers (Germany, Italy and Japan) had little chance of wining the war.	

Dunkirk, May 1940

By the end of May 1940, 225,000 troops of the British Expeditionary Force found themselves encircled and trapped in the French port of Dunkirk by the German army. It seemed that they were bound to be taken prisoner or killed. The German troops were ordered to hold back and the German air force was given the job of 'finishing off' the British and French troops in the town. This was not very effective and over a period of nine days, nearly 340,000 British and French troops were taken off the beaches of Dunkirk by the Royal Navy and ferried back to Britain.

At the time, the evacuation of Dunkirk was greeted as a triumph by the British Press. 'The miracle of Dunkirk' became a common expression. *The Daily Express* wrote this at the time:

> The Army is coming back from Belgium. It is a dirty, tired, hungry army. An army that has been shelled and bombed from three sides, and had to stagger backward into the sea to survive. An army that has been betrayed, but never defeated or dispirited. There was the touch of glory about these returning men as I saw them tramping along a pier, still in formation, still with their rifles. For this army still had a grin on their oily, bearded faces.

Britain in 1940 was fighting for her very survival as a free country. Newspapers tried to show the most depressing of events in the best way possible to keep up morale and the spirit of resistance. But there was another side to Dunkirk which was concealed from the public at the time as this source makes clear:

> When the first groups of the British Expeditionary Force reached Dunkirk on May 27-28 [1940] some of the troops lost their discipline. Armed British naval men had to restore control. Officers also abandoned their men in their rush to get to the boats. General Alexander was shocked at the behaviour of the British troops. On their arrival home in England some troops had such poor morale that 'they threw their rifles and equipment out of the railway carriage windows'... The Ministry of Information told journalists to blame the defeat on French cowardice, while the BEF remained 'undefeated'.

(Adapted from an article by Peter Neville, in *Modern History Review*, 1991)

Huge amounts of equipment had to be abandoned: 475 tanks, 1000 heavy guns and 400 anti-tank guns. In France and Belgium 68,000 British troops had been killed or taken prisoner. The Germans now controlled the whole of the Channel coast and had a good base from which to launch an invasion of Britain.

Your assignment

On the next page is the outline of a newspaper front page with sections for headlines, a report, sketch, and interview with a returning British soldier. You can make up your own newspaper title. This paper is also dated 31st May 1940 (like the Daily Telegraph below) but your task in this assignment is to give a more honest assessment of Dunkirk than the Press could give in May 1940. It is worth remembering that any reference to the events described in the Peter Neville article would have been censored in 1940. For this exercise, we will have to ignore the existence of censorship. The smaller version below is there to show you where the various sections go and gives an example of a possible headline.

This activity is ideally suited to Desk Top Publishing, if you have access to it.

The Battle of Britain

After Dunkirk, Britain faced invasion across the Channel. Before Hitler could transport his troops across the Channel he had to put the RAF out of action, otherwise they would be an easy target for the British pilots. The Battle of Britain refers to this air battle between the RAF and the German air force (the Luftwaffe) for control of the skies.

This exercise will ask you to weigh up the strengths and weaknesses of each of the air forces in the various categories listed below. The text below provides useful information on these strengths and weaknesses.

RAF v Luftwaffe

The Luftwaffe had nearly 2500 planes available for the Battle of Britain: 970 bombers, 340 Stuka dive-bombers, 870 ME 109 fighters and 270 twin-engined ME 110 fighter-bombers. Against this the RAF had 820 fighter planes – the RAF's cause was hopeless from the start, as they were outnumbered 3 to 1 by the Germans.

A closer look at the facts, though, shows a different picture. The Luftwaffe bombers were not a direct threat in the air to the RAF and neither were the Stukas or the ME 110 fighter-bombers. All of these were too slow and cumbersome to take on an RAF Spitfire or Hurricane fighter plane.

The fighters in each air force were more evenly matched. The Spitfire was the best fighter plane at that time. It was faster and had more deadly fire-power than the best German fighter – the ME 109. On the other hand, the ME 109 was faster and more manoeuvrable than the Hurricane, and the Hurricane made up about 550 of the RAF's 820 fighter force.

Most of the German pilots were very experienced. Many had served in the Spanish Civil War in the late–1930s as well as in the victories over Poland and France. British fighter pilots had only seen action over France during the months of May and June, 1940. The German pilots were very confident as a result of their victories but the RAF was fighting to prevent Britain from being invaded.

However, the Luftwaffe pilots were handicapped by the fact that they only had enough fuel for about 20 minutes flying time over south-east England. If they spent any longer over England they risked not having enough fuel to return to their airfields in France. The RAF faced no such difficulties. Furthermore, the RAF also had the benefit of radar which meant the British always knew well in advance when the Luftwaffe were coming, where they were going and how many planes were involved in the attack. This allowed the RAF to 'scramble' their planes and send them directly to intercept the enemy. The Germans did not have radar.

Your assignment

Give each of the two sides, RAF and Luftwaffe, a mark out of ten for each of the six scoring areas listed below. The side with the higher number has the biggest advantage in that area and the closer to ten the more important that area is. Then add up the two totals to see which of the two air forces, on paper, should have won.

In about 250 words explain why you have allocated the scores in the way you have and say which of the six categories you think was the most important in deciding the outcome of the battle.

	RAF	Luftwaffe
Aircraft numbers		
Fighter quality		
Pilot quality		
Pilot morale		
Fuel restrictions		
Value of radar		
Total:		

_____
_____
_____
_____
_____
_____
_____
_____
_____
_____
_____
_____
_____
_____
_____
_____

The Enigma code and the bombing of Coventry

Early in the war, the British military intelligence unit at Bletchley succeeded in breaking the Germans' top secret 'Enigma' code. This allowed them to discover some of enemy's secret plans. In the second week of November, 1940, they intercepted a coded message which ordered the Luftwaffe to destroy Coventry on the night of 14 November. It was to be the biggest German bombing raid of the war: 449 bombers were used.

Churchill was immediately informed of the intended raid. He faced a terrible dilemma. It was vital that the Germans did not find out that the British had broken their secret code. The Germans' aerial reconnaissance would soon find out if any unusual movement around Coventry was taking place. If they saw extra ambulances or anti-aircraft guns being moved to the city a few days before such a massive raid, they would become suspicious.

The alternative was to take no unusual measures and allow Coventry to face the attack with what defences and medical supplies it had.

Your assignment

Write a 250 word report to Churchill putting both points of view, outlining the merits and drawbacks of the two options. Give your recommendation as to what action to take.

The following is a list of points to consider in your report.

- Any unusual activity in the Coventry area would probably tip off the Germans that somehow the British knew of the intended attack.
- They might suspect that their code had been cracked and change it
- Coventry had a population of 300,000.
- It contained 13 vital armaments and engine plants.
- It was particularly poorly defended for such an important industrial and heavily populated city.
- Between a third and a half of the city's population 'trekked' out of the city each night to stay in nearby villages to escape the raids.

What did happen?

The raid took place as expected. About 500 tons of high explosive were dropped on Coventry and 568 people were killed. The casualties were light for such a heavy raid. Many of the population had trekked out that night as was their habit and many others were in shelters. Most of the bombs fell on the city centre in which few people actually lived. One German bomber was shot down.

(It is worth remembering that the RAF, in just four raids over Hamburg in 1943, dropped nearly 9000 tons of explosive and killed 42,000 people.)

What was the war like?

Here are 8 pairs of statements about the war in 1940. One statement in each pair is true. Tick the boxes alongside the correct statements.

☐ **1a** The war was likely to be won by the side with the most industry.

☐ **1b** The war was likely to be won by the side with the most soldiers.

☐ **2a** Aircraft were mainly used for providing information about the enemy.

☐ **2b** Aircraft were mainly used for attacking enemy troops.

☐ **3a** The French defences – the Maginot Line – held up well against the German attack in 1940.

☐ **3b** The Maginot Line proved to be useless against the Germans.

☐ **4a** The Germans were so successful in the early stages of the war because they had the best weapons.

☐ **4b** The Germans were so successful in the early stages of the war because they had the best strategy.

☐ **5a** One reason for the RAF victory in the Battle of Britain was radar.

☐ **5b** One reason for the RAF victory in the Battle of Britain was that the RAF had braver pilots.

☐ **6a** Soldiers in the war spent long periods on the move.

☐ **6b** Soldiers in the war spent long periods in trenches.

☐ **7a** Both sides tried to avoid bombing civilians.

☐ **7b** Both sides bombed civilians.

☐ **8a** Germany lost the war because her soldiers were not brave enough.

☐ **8b** Germany lost the war because her troops were fighting in too many places.

Here is a list of sources which historians might use to find out about the Second World War:

- photographs
- film
- memoirs of generals
- speeches by political leaders
- memoirs of ordinary civilians
- newspapers

- paintings
- weapons
- memoirs of ordinary soldiers
- government records
- popular songs and feature films

1 Choose two sources. Explain what historians might learn from them.

2 In what ways would the memoirs of an ordinary soldier or civilian be different from those of a general or a political leader?

3 In what ways would the memoirs of a general be different to the memoirs of a political leader, like Churchill?

4 Which of the sources above would be of most use to an historian wanting to write about life for the civilian population during the war? Explain what each of these sources would tell an historian.

5 There are far more sources available to an historian of the Second World War than there are for an historian writing about Britain in the Middle Ages. Therefore, historians are more likely to be right about the Second World War than Britain in the Middle Ages.' What is your view of this opinion?

Why did men fight?

The following sources each provide some evidence as to why men were prepared to fight during the war.

1   Why do you think the posters in Source A and B might have encouraged men to fight in the Second World War?

2   What difference can you see in the type of appeal that each of these posters (Sources A and B) is making?

3   Which one of Sources A – F is most like Source G in the message it is putting across? Explain your answer.

4   What similarities and differences can you see in the views expressed in Sources C and F?

5   Of which source do you think the government would most disapprove? Explain your answer.

Source A

Source B

Source C

Ever since your victory at Alamein, you have nightly pitched your tents a day's march nearer home. In the days to come when people ask you what you did in the Second World War, it will be enough to say: I marched with the Eighth Army.

(General Montgomery, 1943

Source D

I went where I was told to go and did what I was told to do, but no more. I was scared witless just about all the time.

(Army private)

Source E

What are we fighting for? Ask any dogface ordinary soldier on the line, you're fighting for your skin on the line. When I enlisted, I was as patriotic as hell. There's no patriotism on the line. A boy up there 60 days in the line is in danger every minute. He ain't fighting for patriotism.

(American soldier)

Source F

There's one thing you men can say when it's all over and you're home once more. You can thank God that twenty years from now when you're sitting by the fireside with your grandson on your knee, and he asks you what you did in the war, you won't have to shift to the other knee, cough and say, I shovelled crap in Louisiana.

(US general, Patton, 1944)

Source G

The German invasion of Russia in June 1941 was the turning point of the war in Europe. Hitler committed 75% of Germany's military might into Barbarossa – the code-name for the attack on Russia. At first the Russians were driven back in confusion. Then they held their ground and from the end of 1942 they began to drive back the Germans and they did not stop until they reached Berlin in April 1945.

Hitler was obsessed with invading Russia. His motives were a confused mixture of politics (the destruction of world communism), race (the Russians were an inferior Slav people) and military factors (oil and wheat for his armies). Leningrad (now St Petersburg) was the centre of Russia's armaments industry; the Ukraine had vast wheat fields and the Caucasus had the oil. In addition, Hitler wanted Moscow, the capital and symbol of Russia.

Army Group North was given Leningrad as its target, Moscow was the target of Army Group Centre, and Army Group South was to head for the Ukraine and then the Caucasus. Later, Stalingrad was added to the list. The addition of Stalingrad was to prove a disastrous error.

Your assignment

The following activities are to be carried out on the photocopied map of the plan of Operation Barbarossa provided by your teacher.

1 Draw three arrows, each representing the course of the attacks by the three Army Groups. Draw an arrow for Army Group North directly to Leningrad, an arrow from AGC through Smolensk but just short of Moscow and an arrow for AGS through Kiev towards the Caucasus. This arrow should divide into two with one part going south to the Caucasus and the other towards Stalingrad.

2 Copy each of the symbols next to the map into the appropriate box on the map itself.

3 Why were the Germans able to launch their invasion from Poland and not Germany?

4 Why do you think diverting part of Army Group South to capture Stalingrad was such a mistake?

5 How does this map help you understand why Russia proved such a difficult country to conquer?

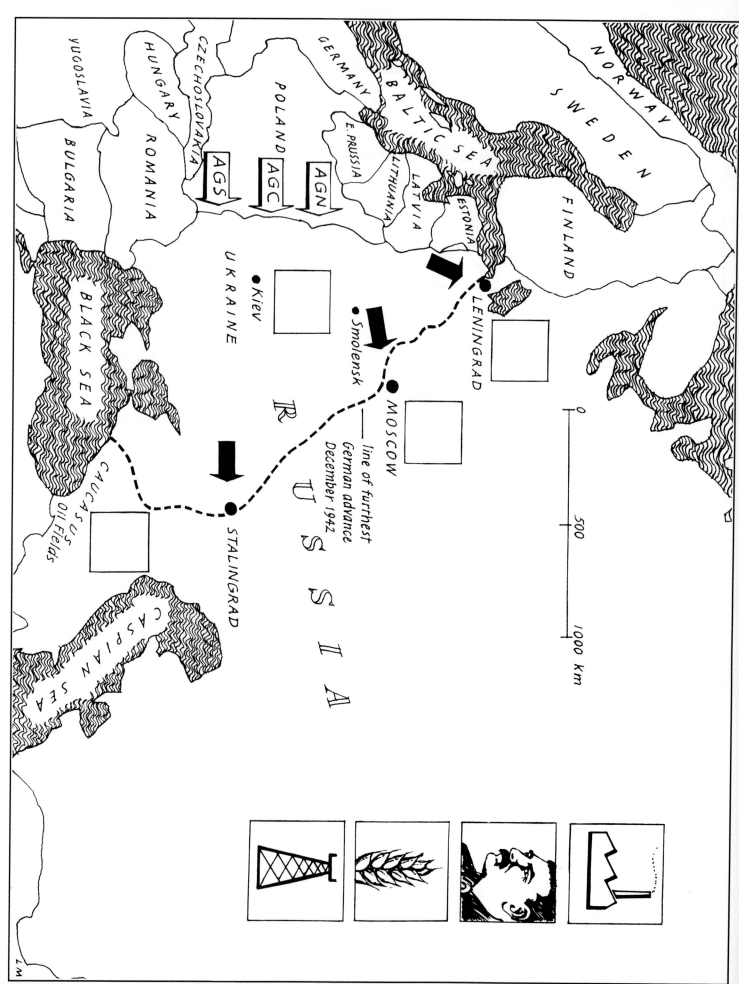

Why did Barbarossa fail?	
Column A: **Reason for defeat**	Column B: **Importance of the reason**
The Russians had a much bigger army than the Germans expected.	Hitler expected that his 'battles of encirclement' strategy would cut off and trap most of the Russian army. But Hitler miscalculated the size of the Soviet army. This mean they had more than enough men to counter-attack – even after hundreds of thousands had been captured in the first months of the war.
The Russians were able to move over 1500 factories away from the fighting.	
The Germans had not expected to be fighting during the winter of 1941/42.	
Hitler attacked too many different targets at the same time.	
The Russians fought with great patriotism to defend the Soviet Union.	
The German attack was delayed by five weeks.	

The treatment of conscientious objectors

Conscientious objectors (COs) are people who refuse to take part in war. Some refused to serve in both the First and Second World Wars because they were pacifists and believed it was morally wrong to kill at any time. Most of these belonged to various Christian groups. Many agreed to serve as 'non-combatants' (stretcher-bearers, cooks, drivers) or to do agricultural work in Britain. Others objected because they were socialists and communists and believed that both wars were being fought for the benefit of the rich at the expense of the workers of Britain and Germany.

1   What evidence is there in Source A that COs were not treated so harshly in the Second World War as they were in the First World War?

2   Can you think of any reasons why there were so many more COs in the Second World War?

3   The existence of women COs in the Second World War was a new development and 24% of them were imprisoned. Why do you think they were so harshly treated and why were there no women COs in the First World War?

4   Cartoons like the one in Source B were fairly common in the Press in the First World War. Do you think it would have been effective in discouraging men from registering as COs? Explain your answer.

5   Cartoons such as the one in Source B were rare in the Second World War and the public was less hostile to conscientious objectors. What reasons can you suggest for this change in attitude?

Source A

In the First World War 16,500 men registered as COs or 'conshies'. Of these, about 5000 were imprisoned for refusing to assist the war effort in any way at all – even as stretcher-bearers or farm workers. In the Second World War, there were about 60,000 men who registered as COs. Of these, 44,000 agreed to work as non-combatants or in agriculture. A total of 3500 were excluded from any war-related service at all. The rest had their cases turned down and, of these, 3000 were imprisoned. One thousand women also registered as COs and 241 were sent to prison.

Source B

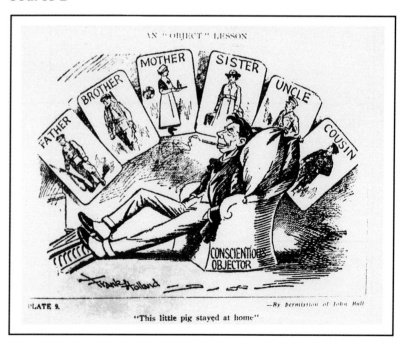

Source A

Aircraft production in 1944. Aircraft were the most important weapon of the war. They could be used to bomb the enemy's industries, railways and dams, as well as their troops and ships.

Allies:	USA	96,000
	Russia	40,000
	Britain	26,000
Axis:	Germany	40,000
	Japan	28,000

Source B

German oil production in millions of barrels (selected months)

1944
May	4.6 m barrels
June	3.0 m barrels
December	1.8 m barrels

1945
March	0.6 m barrels

Note – Allied monthly oil production was about 180 m barrels. At its best German oil production was about 5m barrels a month.

Source C

Source D

Maximum size of the armed forces (army, navy and air forces) during the war. (Note that many of the US forces and some of the British forces would also have fought in the Pacific campaign against Japan and not just against Germany.)

Allies:

Russia	12,500,000
United States	12,400,000
Britain	4,700,000

Axis:

Germany	10,000,000
Japan	6,100,000

Your assignment

Using only the sources on this page, write a 300-word account of why Germany lost the war. Explain which of the reasons you think was most important in bringing about that defeat.

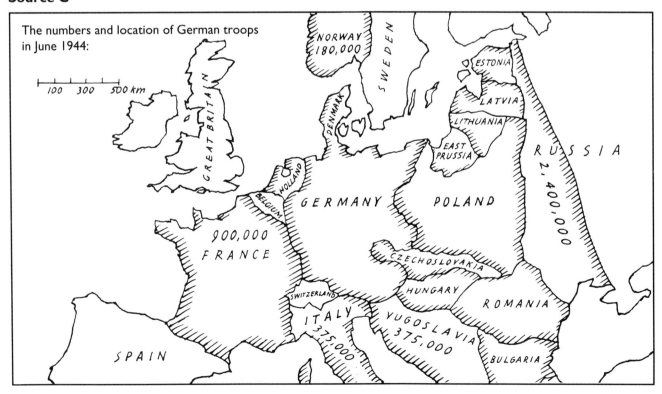

The numbers and location of German troops in June 1944:

100 300 500 km

NORWAY 180,000
SWEDEN
ESTONIA
LATVIA
LITHUANIA
EAST PRUSSIA
RUSSIA 2,400,000
GREAT BRITAIN
DENMARK
HOLLAND
BELGIUM
GERMANY
POLAND
900,000 FRANCE
CZECHOSLOVAKIA
SWITZERLAND
HUNGARY
ROMANIA
ITALY 375,000
YUGOSLAVIA 375,000
BULGARIA
SPAIN

The Japanese naval force of six aircraft carriers and more than two dozen other ships sailed undetected for two weeks and for nearly 6000 kilometres across the North Pacific. The US intelligence service had cracked the Japanese code. They knew that the Japanese navy had asked the Japanese consulate in Hawaii to tell them not only which US ships were in Pearl Harbor (an obvious and usual request) but also where in the harbour they were berthed. That should have aroused suspicions.

The task force reached its destination, 350 kilometres north of Pearl Harbor, on Sunday morning, 7 December. From there, nearly 400 Japanese planes in two waves took off from their carriers to bomb the US Pacific fleet at Pearl Harbor. The surprise attack was devastating and destructive and very well planned. However, what made the raid more effective still were the small 'accidents' of history which on their own do not amount to much. When these small details are put together, however, they become much more important.

Why did the Americans not realize that Pearl Harbor was the target?

- The American commander of the naval base had cancelled weekend reconnaissance flights by his planes in order to save money.
- The Americans had no idea where the Japanese task force was, although they did know it had set sail.
- The United States expected an attack but they also expected Japan to declare war first.
- Radar operators working on the newly installed radar equipment assumed the huge 'blip' on their screen was caused by US planes.

Why was it such a devastating attack?

- The commander of Hawaii, General Short, had ordered all ammunition to be kept locked up and the aircraft to be parked close together to prevent sabotage by Japanese agents.
- The US battle ships were berthed very close together in a row.
- Only 25% of the base's anti-aircraft guns were manned that Sunday morning – the rest had been given the day off.
- The Japanese had trained hard with a new type of torpedo which could be dropped by plane and still work in the shallow waters of the base.

Was Pearl Harbor a Japanese blunder?

- The major target of the attack was the US aircraft carriers. None of these was in Pearl Harbor at the time.
- Five US battleships were sunk but three others were repaired.
- The US ship repair yards and oil storage tanks were not damaged.
- The attack united the whole population of the United States behind the war.

Your assignment

Each of the three questions above has four answers to it. Pick one answer for each of the three questions which you think is the most important and explain why you have chosen it. It will also be necessary to explain why the other answers are less important.

Massacre at Oradour

The event

On Saturday 10 June, 1944, a detachment of 120 troops of the SS division, Das Reich, drove into the sleepy and remote French village of Oradour-sur-Glane. All the inhabitants were told to gather in the main square. A total of 652 men, women and children were then locked up, the men were put into six barns and the women and children into the church. The entire village was set on fire. The men not burned to death in the barns were machine gunned. The church was also set alight and grenades were thrown in through windows.

In the massacre 245 women, 207 children and 190 men perished: 642 in total since 10 managed to escape. In 1953 a French court sentenced 20 of the SS men to death but only two were executed. The village was never rebuilt and still stands today, in ruins, as a memorial to its victims.

Why did it happen?

Until the late 1980s there was no serious disagreement among historians as to why the massacre took place – though there are differences:

Source A

The people were told by the commandant that explosives were reported to have been hidden in the village and that a search and checking of identity cards would be made.

(W. Shirer, The Rise and Fall of the Third Reich, 1959)

Source C

They were locked in the village church, and then killed as a reprisal [revenge] for the killing of an SS man by French partisans in a distant village, but one with the same name.

(M. Gilbert, Holocaust, 1986)

Source B

They [the villagers] had committed no crimes but were the helpless victims of the SS which had been unable to find one of its commanders kidnapped by the French Maquis [resistance]. The SS division had also been harassed by French Resistance fighters.

(R. Goralski, World War Two Almanac, 1981)

Study the sources above and answer the following.

1 Which two of these sources have most in common regarding the reason for the massacre? Explain your answer.
2 How do you suppose these historians were able to put together their account of the massacre?

The massacre at Oradour was filed away for over 40 years as one of many atrocities. There did not seem to be any reason for further investigation since there was no dispute as to what happened that June day. However, in the late-1980s a book was published which was to cause some controversy – not about what happened buy why it happened.

Enter Robin Mackness, 1988

In 1982, an English businessman, Robin Mackness, learnt something which he was convinced blew apart the accepted version of events and the reasons behind them. He decided to test his new theory to see if it could answer any of the questions which he believed the existing theories could not answer. He claimed that there were six questions about the massacre which the traditional, accepted view of historians could not answer (see below).

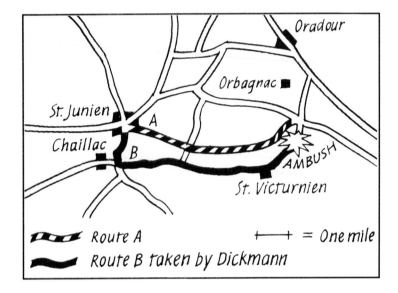

Mackness' questions

a Why was Oradour – a town with no history of resistance activity chosen for this reprisal?

b Why did the SS not publicize the massacre afterwards as a warning to others not to support the Resistance fighters?

c Why was the officer in charge, Major Dickmann, so enraged when he discovered that the men held in the sixth barn had already been killed before he could question them?

d Why were two local pro-Nazi Frenchmen, acting as interpreters, also shot on Dickmann's orders at the end of the reprisal?

e Why were the inhabitants of Oradour ordered off a train which arrived from Limoges during the afternoon while the people from Limoges were allowed to return to their town?

f Why did Dickmann, on the morning of 10 June, take route B from St Junien to Oradour rather than the more direct route A (see map)? Route A was quicker and less likely to be ambushed by the local Resistance fighters.

3 Is there anything in the account you have read so far which could help you answer any of Mackness' 'unanswered' questions?

The Mackness theory

In 1982 Mackness was arrested by the French customs for smuggling gold into the country and spent 12 months in a French prison. Mackness claimed a man called Raoul had asked him to smuggle the gold. Raoul told him that the gold had originally belonged to the SS 'Das Reich' division. Mackness would not reveal the identity of Raoul.

Raoul said that on the night of 9 June, 1944, he and six other Resistance fighters ambushed a three-vehicle column of the SS after midnight. All but one of the Germans was killed – he escaped in the darkness. Raoul was the only survivor from the Resistance. Inside one of the trucks he discovered 30 shoe-box sized crates of gold. During the rest of the night. Raoul buried the crates of gold, worth perhaps £6 million in today's value. The escaped German reported the ambush to Major Dickmann on the road to Oradour.

After his release from prison, Mackness was determined to find out if Raoul's story could be true. Dickmann could tell Mackness nothing. He had been killed in action a few days after the massacre. He asked the local inhabitants about the ambush that night 9 June, 1944. No one knew anything of it. Neither did the Resistance files have any record of such an attack. According to Raoul, who had died in 1984, the ambush had taken place on the road from St. Julien to Oradour, about four kilometres to the south of Oradour. The gold had been looted by Dickmann's troops during the course of their activities in France and Dickmann wanted it back. He was convinced the gold must still be in the area.

4 Using Mackness' theory, answer the six questions above which he claimed the traditional view could not answer.

5 Suggest three reasons why an historian might not be satisfied with Mackness' account?

6 What difficulties would an historian now have in trying to check this account of events?

The historian and new evidence

New evidence about the past often leads historians to change totally their earlier opinions. When an historian is faced with new 'evidence' about the past, he should ask three basic questions:

- Does the new evidence make sense?

- Does it fit in with what is already known to be true?

- Does the new evidence fill in any gaps in the existing evidence?

One historian, M.R.D. Foot, in his review of Mackness' book, *Oradour, Massacre and Aftermath*, wrote: 'Much of "Oradour" is highly improbable, verging sometimes on the ridiculous, hardly any of it is provably wrong'.

7 What is your view of the Mackness version of the events of 9-10 June, 1944?

What happened when?

In this exercise there are seven cartoons. Each cartoon comes from a different year of the war, beginning in 1939 and ending in 1945: one cartoon for each year. There are clues in the cartoons which link the cartoon to a particular event in that year. For example, the cartoon below shows Hitler being crushed inside a copy of his book, Mein Kampf and another Nazi (Himmler) waving a white flag. Clearly Germany has been defeated and the war is almost over so the date must be 1945. Once you have sorted all the cartoon letters into the right order, explain why you have linked each cartoon to a particular year.

1939 ....

1940 ....

1941 ....

1942 ....

1943 ....

1944 ....

1945 ....

THE LAST CHAPTER

Cartoon A

THE GAMBLER'S BIGGEST BET

Cartoon B

EAST OR WEST?

Cartoon C

"SCRAM!"

Cartoon D

"Here you are! Don't lose it again!"

Cartoon E

RENDEZVOUS

OVERSHADOWED   —by Illingworth.

'IT IS REPORTED THAT GERMANY WILL RECONSTITUTE THE FASCIST GOVERNMENT IN NORTH ITALY.

" DUCE ! DUCE ! "

1   In the 'Men and Women' column of the grid, write the names of these people in the correct boxes. They should be in chronological order and are connected to the other people or events on the grid.

William the Conqueror	David Livingstone	George Stephenson
Charles I	Athelstan	Louis Pasteur
Boudicca	Hadrian	Richard Arkwright
Oliver Cromwell	Queen Elizabeth I	W. E. Gladstone
King John	Julius Caesar	

2   In the 'Peoples and Dynasties' column write the names of these groups of people in the correct boxes.

Normans   Tudors   Celts   Victorians   Stuarts   Saxons

3   In the 'Events' column write these events in the correct boxes, linking them to the people or dynasties they are connected with.

Domesday Book	Start of the Church of England
English Civil War	Railways and vaccinations against
Rebellions against the Romans	disease
Wars of the Roses	Votes for all men
Magna Carta	Battle of Hastings

Men and Women	Peoples and Dynasties	Events
Caratacus		
	Romans	Building of towns, roads and a great wall in the north
Alfred the Great		England becomes one country after the Viking attacks
Richard III	Plantagenets	
Henry VIII		Defeat of the Armada
		11 years without a king
Thomas Telford	Hanoverians	Industrial Revolution
Disraeli		Growth of British Empire

1   Look at Resources cards 25-32
    These cards show people or scenes from different periods of British history. Match the cards to the correct period by writing the numbers of the cards in the correct circles below.

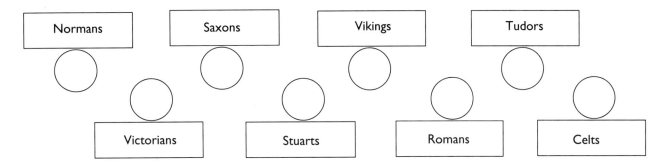

2   Place the cards in chronological order and write the names of each period on the timeline below.

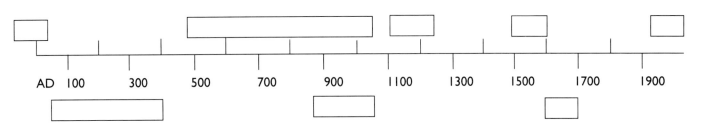

3   You might have had difficulty with activities 1 and 2 because some periods were very similar. Which periods were very much like each other?

4   What name is given to the period between AD500 and AD1500?

5   Which events mark the beginning and the end of this period?

Early modern Britain

1 Below are four boxes containing the numbers of Resource cards. These cards show scenes from the periods of history shown below.

   Medieval   Tudor   Stuart   Industrial Revolution

   a In the boxes shade the scenes from the Tudor period.

   b Put a cross through the boxes showing scenes from the Stuart period.

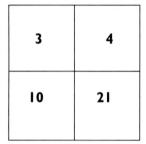
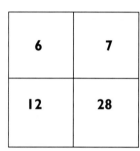
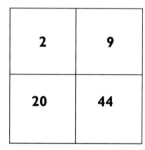
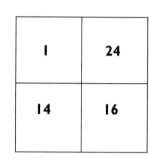

1200   2000

2 Mark on the timeline below the Tudor and Stuart periods.

3 Which developments or inventions did people in Tudor and Stuart England find new and exciting?

4 If you went back in time to early modern England what would you find most strange or difficult or uncomfortable?

5 Which events or inventions mark the end of the Middle Ages and the beginning of early modern England?

Activity 1

a Below you can see the numbers of a set of Resource cards. Shade the numbers of the cards that show events that took place during the Industrial Revolution.

| 9 | 12 | 14 | 16 | 19 | 20 | 21 | 22 | 24 | 35 | 42 | 43 |

b Mark on the timeline below the period when the Industrial Revolution occurred.

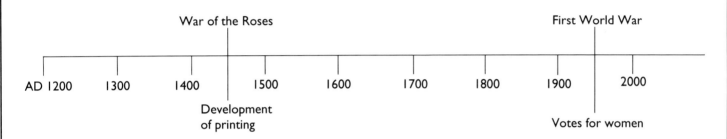

Activity 2

a Look at your answers to Activity 1. Do you think people at the time of the Industrial Revolution felt that it was a time of great and rapid change? Explain your answer

b Look at the Resource cards showing developments during the Industrial Revolution. Do you think that these developments made people's lives better or worse? Explain your answer.

The modern world

You will need Resource cards 10, 16, 19, 21, 22, 24, 33, 34, 36, 40, 42, 44.

These cards show changes that have happened in the last 500 years: 4 were changes at the time of the Renaissance, 4 from the Industrial Revolution and 4 from the twentieth century. Which cards belong to which time? Write the card numbers in the correct circles below.

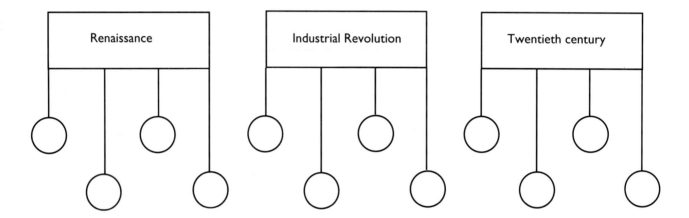

Can you see any connections between these events and changes? Look at the cards numbered in the boxes, then write your explanation of why these changes were connected.

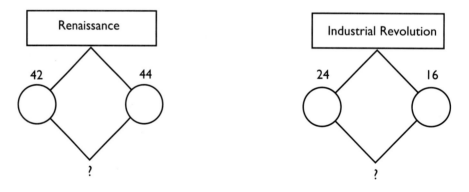

Can you work out any more connections for yourself? Which of these times of change saw the greatest changes? Explain your answer.

Modern world events

Activity 1

a Below you can see the numbers of a set of Resource cards. Put the numbers of the cards in the correct place on the timeline.

14   15   18   22   23   33   36   37   38   40   43

b One card shows an event that happened before this period. Shade that card's number.

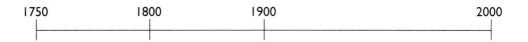

| 1750 | 1800 | 1900 | 2000 |

Activity 2

Here you can see two lists, one of people and another of events. Write the names of the people next to the events they were involved in.

Neil Armstrong   Lenin

Mao Zedong   Churchill

Napoleon   Hitler

Wellington   Gandhi

Martin Luther King   E. Pankhurst

George Washington   Pasteur

The Battle of Waterloo	
Civil rights in USA	
Prime Minister in World War II	
Votes for women	
French domination of Europe	
The Russian Revolution	

American War of Independence	
The rise of the Nazi party	
The Chinese Revolution	
Indian independence	
Moon landing	
Discovery of germ theory	

Activity 3

Cards 22, 33, 36, 39, 41 and 43 show events in modern history. Which of these events was the most important? Explain your answer or choose another event altogether!

33

34

The art of Leonardo De Vinci
Painting and sculpture became much more realistic

35

European voyages to America led by Columbus, Cabot,
Hawkins

36

The Russian Revolution when the tsar was overthrown

37

The American War of Independence – America fought against
Britain to win her freedom

38

Louis Pasteur and germ theory – after this discovery
diseases like cholera could be conquered

39

Computers

40

The invention of aeroplanes by the Wright Brothers

41

The development of nuclear power

42

The invention of printing

43

The Second World War

44

The Reformation: The beginning of Protestant Churches which broke away from the Roman Catholic Church